Year Round Healthy Holiday Dishes

Plant Based Recipes

By Valerie Wilson

ISBN – 9781083098368

© 2019 Valerie Wilson

All rights reserved. No part of this book may used or reproduced by any means, graphic, electronic or mechanical, including photocopying, recording, taping or by any information storage retrieval system without the written permission of the publisher except in the case of brief quotations embodied in reviews.

The author of this book does not dispense medical advice or prescribe the use of any technique as a form of treatment for physical, emotional, or medical condition either directly or indirectly. The intent of the author and information provided herein is only to offer information of a general nature to help you in your quest for your over-all wellbeing. In the event that you use any of this information in this book for yourself, which is your constitutional right, the author and the publisher assume no responsibility for your actions.

All recipes, poetry and photographs are the personal and intellectual property of Valerie Wilson.

Other books by Valerie Wilson include:
Healthy and Delicious Cooking Spring Season
Perceptions in Healthy Cooking Revised Edition
Vegan Cooking with Kids Fun Recipes for Children

Dedication

This book is dedicated to my grandmother, Marguerite Wilson Buck. She was a great cook and made the best pies. She was outgoing, adventurous and loved the outdoors, all qualities I am proud to have inherited. My grandmother rode horses, motorcycles, drove large tractor on her farm, went camping, helped run a Girl Scout troop, and raised three very active wonderful sons, one being my father. She was an actively involved Grandmother in my life, especially when I was young. She was there to see me march in parades in both band and Girl Scouts, and always on birthdays and holidays. I will always remember when she attended one of my cooking classes, it is a cherished memory.

She and my grandfather owned a large farm in Carney, in the Upper Peninsula of Michigan. My first time there I was just a baby. The picture is of me as a baby at my grandparent's farm. Grandma is holding an apple, which seems fortuitous to me. My love affair with the U.P. of Michigan started at an early age. Many of my childhood holidays were spent at their farm and influence my ideas about celebrate the holidays, to this day. I mention the farm and the Upper Peninsula often in this book. I started writing this cookbook while she was still on this earth and she was very excited to hear about the book. She is no longer here physically, but I know she is with me, supporting me, and loving me, just in a different way.

Special Thanks:

To my parents who have loved and supported me throughout my life and on my journey to teaching healthy cooking.

My sister, Laura Wilson, for all her help in running my website and all the work she does to help me in my business.

My brother, Peter Wilson, for helping to proofread the cookbook.

To all my regular students who have attended my cooking classes and encourage me to keep creating new recipes.

To all my customers who get to be my taste testers as I work on perfecting the recipes I have created.

To Mike Max Maxwell for the marketing ideas.

To Dawn Follis for all her support and help in my business. And for being the photographer who took the cover picture

To Marie Oser for writing the foreword and all her editing help.

Table of Contents

Foreword	VII
About Val Page	VIII
Introduction	1
Thanksgiving	21
Christmas Dinner	29
Holiday Goodies	39
New Year's Eve	49
Valentine's Day	61
Easter	71
Mother's Day	81
Memorial Day	91
Father's Day	101
Fourth of July	111
Labor Day	121
Halloween	131
Glossary	142
Index	144

Foreword

Valerie Wilson is the kind of grass roots, plant based advocate that reaches people on a personal level with enticing food and important information regarding plant based nutrition and healthful ingredients.

In addition to posting videos to YouTube, Macro Val, as she is known in vegan communities on the Internet is a personal chef and cooking class instructor. She produces a podcast, Real Food with Chef Val that features information on plant based nutrition and a popular 'Recipe of the Month' segment. Valerie appears at farmers markets regularly.

In this latest book, Year Round Healthy Holiday Dishes, her message of promoting healthful, low fat and antioxidant rich plant based cookery is underscored in festive and delicious dishes that are perfect for the holiday table or at any time of year.

Marie Oser, best-selling author and executive producer of VegTV, www.vegtv.com

Chef Valerie Wilson, also known as Macro Val, has been in the food industry since 1985. She has been living a vegan, macrobiotic whole foods lifestyle since 1993. She started teaching cooking classes in 1997 and still teaches in South Eastern Michigan. She is the author of three other cookbooks: ***Perceptions in Healthy Cooking Revised Edition***, ***Healthy and Delicious Cooking Spring Season***, and ***Vegan Cooking with Kids Fun Recipes for Children***. Since 2012 she has hosted radio shows and is currently the host of her own podcast, **REAL FOOD with Chef Val**. She offers in person and over the phone *Lifestyle Counseling Sessions* where she has helped people overcome health challenges such as: arthritis, allergies, diabetes, and cancer.

Chef Val is also a personal chef who will come cook for you at your home and offers in home cooking classes at your home for individuals or groups.

Chef Val has been a regular writer for the ***Health and Happiness*** magazine based in the Upper Peninsula of Michigan since 1999. You can watch her informative videos on her YouTube channel and follow her on Facebook, Macro Val Food. For contact information and links to all her services, www.macroval.com

Introduction

I love cooking for the holidays. Whether Thanksgiving, Christmas, Easter or Memorial Day, there is something special about creating healthy, delicious dishes to share with family and friends at holiday celebrations. My intention for this cookbook is to have healthy recipes for all the holidays throughout the year. The recipes in this cookbook are some of my most flavorful and distinct dishes.

In 1997 I started teaching cooking classes after working at a Macrobiotic cooking school for two years. My goal was to create a fun environment where people could learn how to use healthy, whole ingredients to create delicious dishes. Many of my classes have holiday themes and Valentine's Day was one of my first holiday cooking classes. I am inspired to teach recipes that reflect the time of year and traditional foods associated with a particular holiday. Family recipes and how my family celebrated holidays influence my interpretation in many of these dishes. I share some of my personal stories throughout this book and recreating how my family celebrated the holidays has made this work all the more enjoyable.

Holidays are, for the most part, associated with family and cultural traditions and there are many ways to celebrate. Holiday recipes can be a melting pot of different cultures, foods and families. In my family we had many special recipes that my mom would make for Christmas that I learned from her when I was young. When I changed to a macrobiotic, vegan lifestyle, I took many of those recipes and converted ingredients to make them healthier and plant based. It gives me great pleasure to serve delicious and healthy versions of my favorite childhood holiday dishes. And everyone seems to love them too.

Holiday dishes should be colorful, because we eat with our eyes first and looking to nature, holiday dishes should reflect the colors of the season. Mother's Day dishes have very bright vibrant colors to reflect the colorful spring season. Fourth of July dishes are also very colorful for the summer season. Holidays in the fall, such as Halloween, have more brown and earthy tones and include pumpkins and root vegetables. Winter holidays are pretty much the most popular. Thanksgiving and Christmas have earth tones in the ingredients with many colorful garnishes to accent the darker colors. Chopped parsley is a popular garnish to finish off a festive holiday dish. When you use healthy, whole ingredients from Mother Earth that have not been sprayed with chemicals, altered, refined or processed you can create wonderfully delicious, colorful, festive dishes for every holiday.

Whole Grains

Whole grains are the staple of a healthy diet. All our ancestors, no matter where you are from, had a diet based in a type of whole grains. It is what is missing in the average American diet. Start eating whole grains every day and you will see a huge difference in the way you feel. Whole grains have been eaten for tens of thousands of years and recent studies have found it could be up to a hundred thousand years. They are the seeds of plants in which the main source of nutrition comes from the outer shell of the grain, called the **bran** and **germ**. These whole grains are what gives the body energy. When eaten, they release glucose very slowly into the body. This gives you long, sustainable energy to last all day long. Very high in fiber, also high in B vitamins, whole grains have also been studied for their anti cancer properties.

The human body is designed to eat and assimilate whole grains. In your mouth you have 32 teeth: 4 canine, 8 incisors and 20 molars. These molars are the majority of the teeth, designed to grind whole grains, indicating the majority of your food should consist of whole grains.

There are three main sources of nutrition for the human body: carbohydrates, protein and fats. Only two of these gives you energy, carbohydrates and fat. The carbs need to be in their whole form or whole grains. Take the bran and germ away, where all the nutritional value resides, and what you have left is simple carbohydrates. These simple carbs is what the majority of people are eating in our modern culture. This confusion as to what an actual whole grain is has become a dangerous trend of cutting out carbs from our diet. We cannot cut out the complex carbs. To have a balanced diet and live a pain free, disease free life you have to eat all three important nutrients: carbs, protein, and fat.

Whole grains are not an ingredient in a box cereal, crackers, or a loaf of bread. They come in the bulk section of health food stores. They look like little seeds. Flour made from whole grains can be a healthy part of your diet, but are not whole grains. Once you grind the grains they react differently in your digestive system. Here is a list of whole grains: **amaranth, barley, brown rice, corn, kasha or buckwheat, millet, quinoa, rolled oats, spelt, faro, rye and whole wheat.**

Amaranth is one of the signature whole grains of the summer. It is very small and that makes it challenging to cook. I have found it is most flavorful if you cook it with other grains. It also has a tendency to be thick and gooey when cooked. This makes it ideal to add to oatmeal and make a breakfast porridge. Amaranth was the sacred food of the Aztecs. Wherever this whole grain is consumed there is little or no mal-nutrition. One plant will yield 50 thousand seeds. It is related to quinoa, the other signature grain of summer. But unlike quinoa that falls apart after it is cooked, which makes it great for salads, amaranth remains thick and creamy making it good for other things, such as porridges.

Amaranth is in a group of plants known as photosynthetic super formers. This makes it above normal in efficiently converting soil, sunlight, and water into plant tissue. Making it have extraordinary nutritional value. High in Vit. A, B6, K, C, Folate and riboflavin. Rich in minerals, iron, calcium, potassium, and manganese. Amaranth is very high in protein, fiber and amino acids.

Barley is the whole grain known for cleansing the body and one of the signature whole grains of spring. It is one of the oldest grains originating in Southwest Asia around 8500 B.C. Roasted barley was one of the main food of the gladiators because it gives tremendous strength when eaten. Known for strengthening the blood and intestines, barley contains potassium, iron, calcium, protein, and fiber. When buying barley, look for whole barley. Pearl barley has the bran polished off, which loses the fiber and other nutrients. Barley is excellent for soups, stews, salads, and added to vegetable dishes. It has a chewy, creamy texture, and a nice sweet taste. If you have gluten sensitivities, substitute brown rice for any recipe using barley.

Brown rice is the mother of all whole grains, meaning it is the superior and most nutrient of the whole grains. It is the signature whole grain of fall. High in fiber to help flush out all the excess stored un-digested food in your intestinal tract. It acts like a big broom to help cleanse the intestines. And contains a wide range of antioxidants to help fight off diseases in the body. Here is a list of some of them:
-Polysaccharides to stimulate immunity and control blood sugar levels
-Oil in rice bran to counteract cholesterol excess
-Many B vitamins to help body deal with stress
-Coenzyme Q 10 to help improve heart health and treat migraine headaches. Burns fat into energy and therefore reduces obesity.
-Gamma-oryzanol, found only in rice bran, it strengthens the musculature of the body while converting fat to lean body mass. It improves hormonal balance through regulation of the pituitary secretion.

Helps improve blood circulation to the extremities and can help overcome clots and blood stagnation in general.
-Superoxide dismutase helpful in treating cataracts, rheumatoid and osteoarthritis.
-Proanthocyanidins help facilitate wound healing, strengthen the arteries, veins and capillaries and improve blood circulation. Most potent antioxidants available to help protect against cancer and most other degenerative diseases. Plus protect against poisons and toxins in the body's lymph and organ systems.
-Lecithin are fatty substances containing phosphorus. It is especially important for proper functioning of the brain and enhancing activity of the brain, plus it appears to improve attention and learning in children. Greatly helps increase absorption of fat-soluble vitamins such as vitamin A. Lecithin also protect against gallstone formation, high blood pressure, and cholesterol excesses.
-IP6 has strong anti-cancer properties. Also used in treating cardiovascular disease, and kidney stones. IP6 is essentially the phytic acid in brown rice that has been shown to somewhat provoke a cleansing therapy for the body.

Basically brown rice is one of the most healing, super foods on the planet and if you want to start on a path of living a healthy lifestyle, consuming brown rice is your first step.

Corn is not your favorite vegetable, it is one of the signature whole grain of the summer. Energetically it feeds your brain and heart, your two most active organs in your body. It was the most widely used whole grain for the Native Americans and still one of the most popular grains consumed in the summer. It can strengthen your overall energy and helps strengthen your blood, stomach and bladder. Corn can help lower blood sugar levels and help prevent urinary stones from forming. It is the only whole grains to contain vitamin A. Corn is a great addition to any whole grain salad or soup.

Kasha, also known as ***buckwheat***, is the signature grain of winter. It is probably the most unknown and under rated of the whole grains. Having a creamy texture and a unique robust flavor it can be very satisfying used in a hearty winter meal. It is a staple food in the very cold Siberia, also where it originated. Even though it has 'wheat' in its name, it is not in the wheat family and it is completely gluten free. Containing the bioflavonoid rutin makes it medicinal for the capillaries and blood vessels, thus increasing circulation to the hands and feet. In Oriental medicine it is said to feed and nurture the kidneys, adrenals, and reproductive organs.

Some other wonderful things about kasha:
- high proportions of all eight essential amino acids
- contains almost the entire range of B-complex vitamins
- 100% more calcium than other grains
- stabilizes blood sugar levels.

You will have a couple of options when buying kasha. The toasted variety has been toasted already. It has a nutty taste and cooks quicker than the untoasted. Kasha that is not toasted is sometimes called 'raw'. Both are very delicious and can be used to make a morning porridge, casseroles, soups, stir fries, and patties. Kasha that is ground into flour is then called buckwheat, which makes great pancakes.

Millet is most recognizable as the small, round, yellow seed in bird feed. It should be recognized as the incredibly healthy whole grain to promote a long life. Very high in fiber, making it a heart healthy food and can help lower cholesterol. Also has a good amount of iron, calcium, potassium, zinc, phosphorus, manganese, and magnesium. Interesting to note, millet has the highest protein content of the whole grains, 11%. Energetically, millet feeds and nurtures your spleen, pancreas and stomach. The main organs that help you deal with stress, so millet is your anti-stress grain.

Millet is creamy, nutty, and slightly sweet, and is the signature whole grain for late summer. Millet has the highest amino acid protein profile and highest iron content. It is a gluten-free grain and contains B vitamins, also rich in phosphorus. Millet is the easiest whole grain to digest and is alkalizing to the body. The first written reference to millet is dated 2800 B.C. Frequently noted in the New Testament, millet flourished throughout the Roman Empire and into the Middle Ages. It is the main food of the Huza people in Asia. They are known for their long lives.

When cooking with millet, it will cook up creamy. It works well to thicken soups and as a casserole. Look for millet in the bulk section or pre-package section of your local health store.

Quinoa (pronounced 'keen-wa') was the mother grain of the Incas. They considered it sacred and held ceremonies honoring quinoa. In South America, in the high altitudes of the Andes Mountains, quinoa has been grown, harvested, and eaten since at least 3,000 B.C. Because of its hardiness, being able to survive at such high altitudes, quinoa is considered a strengthening food.

Although botanically quinoa is a fruit, we classify it as a whole grain. In fact, quinoa is one of the signature whole grains for summer. As one of the easiest whole grains to digest, it gives us a tremendous amount of energy to be able to be very active in the summertime. Quinoa is high in calcium, phosphorus, iron, vitamin E, magnesium, and manganese and is a complete protein. Quinoa is high in quercetin and kaempferol, two flavonoids that have anti-inflammatory, anti-viral, anti-cancer and anti-depressant properties.

Quinoa cooks up quickly and has a nutty flavor, making it ideal for creating cold salads, perfect for a summer meal.

Rolled Oats is one of my favorites and I use it in many diverse ways in my recipes. Traditionally grown in cold damp climates, it was the staple grain for the Celts. Oats contain a healthy fat content that makes it ideal to help impart stamina and warmth in your body. It is one of the signature whole grains of spring. This whole grain can help stabilize blood sugar levels, regulate the thyroid, sooth digestive system, and help reduce high cholesterol.

Rolled oats make great cookies, can be used to thicken soups, sauces and makes a great topping for fruit crisps. Oat flour is the best gluten free flour to create cakes, cookies and baked goods.

Spelt is an ancient red wheat whole grain. A staple in the diets of the Middle Eastern Mediterranean area for over 9,000 years. It became available in America in 1980 which means it has not been contaminated the way whole wheat has been. Many people who have difficulties digesting whole wheat do not have any problem digesting spelt. It is high in zinc, iron, manganese, magnesium, B vitamins, and vitamin E and has phosphorus, protein and fatty acids.

Spelt flour is great for all your baking needs. It make your cakes, muffins and breads light, moist and holds the baked goods together. Spelt does contain gluten.

Whole wheat has received a bad rap lately with the gluten free craze that is going on in our culture. Most people who think they have a gluten problem, usually have a refined white flour problem messing with their digestion and creating many health issues. (Unless you have celiac disease.) Plus our wheat crops are sprayed with so many chemicals that could be the reason many people have a problem with wheat. Most often the health issues people suffer from are caused by the chemicals sprayed on our food. It is very important to buy organic whole wheat. If you have a strong digestion then choosing an organic whole wheat flour for your dishes can be a healthy nutritious choice. Whole wheat contains B vitamins, folic acid, calcium, phosphorus, zinc copper iron and very high in fiber. Whole wheat and spelt are two of the signature whole grains of spring.

Arsenic in brown rice... the real story

    Arsenic in rice? That is all that is on the news TV today. Do people listen to this information and believe it? I sure hope not. Yesterday it was arsenic in apple juice. Now to get the attention off of other subjects (like obesity from junk foods) let's find another healthy food and confuse the public even more. Please, please do not feed into the fear. Do not fall into this *misdirecting of our attention* trap. We live in a culture where we tell a story before we have all the facts. We live in a fear based culture where some of us have lost our common sense.
    First let's look at history. Brown rice has been eaten for thousands of years. It is the staple food for more than half the population on the planet. If these "supposed" high levels of arsenic were in rice, why have we not had a problem way, way, before now? They have reported high levels of arsenic can be a cause of some cancers (again feeding on our fears). Why then has our cancer epidemic only been happening in the last 50 to 60 years after the introduction of refined, processed, and chemically sprayed foods? Also genetically engineered foods, maybe this hoopla has all come out to scare people to accepting some genetically engineered form of 'arsenic resistant' rice the big chemical companies are trying to get into our food chain And to imply that rice consumption has anything to do with cancer is absurd! Brown rice is one of the most nutritional foods on the planet.
    In Paul Pitchford's book *Healing With Whole Foods*, there is a four page section that lists all the health benefits of brown rice from B vitamins to multiple antioxidant properties. Here is a direct quote from the book:

"Additional healing values of brown rice extracts for immune strengthening are being tested. One of the most potent compounds for stimulating NK (natural killer) cells in the body is polysaccharide composed of the hemicellulose-B extract from rice bran, which has been modified by enzymes of the shiitake mushroom. One NK cell can destroy up to 27 cancer cells, taking just a few minutes for each eradication. NK cells are also noted for overcoming dangerous viruses such as hepatitis C and HIV. This shiitake enzyme modified rice bran extract (known as 'MGN-3' can increase NK cell activity from 100 to 500%. Such as increase in immune response has led to some remarkable effects on nearly all pathology indicators, including tumor reduction as well as remission of disease."

If we are looking for a culprit for our cancer epidemic maybe we should look to chicken. The FDA admits that 98% of chicken consumed have cancer. If the flesh you are consuming has cancer, your flesh will develop cancer. And if you are looking for where we are getting high levels of arsenic, 75% of the chickens consumed have high levels of arsenic in them. The arsenic is in their food. Why is that not being discussed on the TV?

And did you know there are different types of arsenic? There is the organic type that is found in nature, and inorganic type that is from manmade chemicals. These chemicals are in the pesticides that have been sprayed on our crops. The chemical residue is now in the soil. Which is why the apple juices that had the highest levels of arsenic in them were from other countries that sprayed their crops more than we do. And the organic arsenic is found in some mineral supplements in small quantities because it occurs naturally in soil.

This whole scare tactic about brown rice started was from an article in *Consumers Report*. I have read the report in the November 2012 issue of *Consumer Report* magazine. As I suspected, there is only one sentence in the article that tells the whole story: **"Meharg, a leading researcher in the field, noted the Department of Agriculture has invested in research to breed types of rice that can withstand arsenic."**

Protein Foods

Protein is essential in our diets to create a healthy life. Protein is in every cell of our bodies and responsible for cell replication. It is required for the structure, function and regulation of the body's tissues and organs, plus building and repairing body tissues. Protein plays an important role in our diets, but will never give you energy. Carbohydrates and fats give you energy. You do have to use caution with protein because the over consumption of protein foods can result in an accumulation of urea, uric acid, fat, and cholesterol in the body, tissues and blood.

When asked where you get protein in a vegan diet, my response is: "Everything that grows out of the ground from Mother Earth in its whole form, contains some protein." Some foods have more than others and even fruit has a small amount of protein. Vegan foods that are exceptionally high in protein are:
-All types of beans
-All soybean foods
-All dark leafy greens
-All sea vegetables
-All nuts and seeds
-Quinoa
-Millet
-All mushrooms, especially shiitakes.

Fats

Fats in your diet are important to help give you energy and support cell growth. Good quality unsaturated fats can help some nutrients get absorbed, keep the body warm, protect organs, and help produce important hormones. Olive oil is considered the healthies fat to consume. It is a monounsaturated fat and helps reduce bad cholesterol, lower risks of heart disease and stroke.

Polyunsaturated fats are also good quality unsaturated fats. That includes; sunflower seeds, walnuts, flax seeds, safflower oil, other plant based oils and other nuts as well. Saturated fats, on the other hand, are best to be avoided.

Brown Rice Syrup

When asked what is my favorite sweetener to use I always answer, brown rice syrup. Unfortunately most people have not heard of it, which makes it the best kept health food secret. I make all kinds of desserts with brown rice syrup, from cookies, cakes, and pies, to candies, fudge, jams, and so much more. As the name implies, it is made from brown rice, which is a whole grain, a complex carbohydrate, a staple in all of our ancestor's diet. The brown rice syrup is produced when naturally occurring enzymes convert the starch in the grain to sugar. The process retains the vitamin and mineral content of the brown rice. And being made from a complex carbohydrate, the sugar that is produced is maltose.

Maltose is the least reactive sugar there is, it releases slowly into your blood stream. Unlike white sugar or sucrose which releases very quickly into the blood stream and wreaks havoc with all the organs in your body. Brown rice syrup and the maltose in the syrup will not spike your blood sugar. For that reason it is considered the healthiest sweetener.

It has a mild sweet taste that is satisfying. However, if you have been using sweeteners that are very sweet, it may not be sweet enough for you at first. If you stick with the brown rice syrup, it will taste sweet after you give up all those intensely sweet foods that are not good for you. You can find it in a jar at you local health food store, or even some main stream grocery stores now carry it. It is thick and sticky like honey.

Soy, the ridicules controversy…

Often while teaching a cooking class I get asked if soy food is good for you. I believe there is a lot of misleading information that causes many people to become confused. When considering what foods are good for us and what may not be, I look to history. If a food has been eaten for a long time, and with no problems, we can know it is safe for us to eat. Such is the case with soy. Five thousand year old texts describe soybeans as being one of the most important crops grown. Miso, fermented soybeans, has been eaten since 2,500 years ago in China. And tempeh has been eaten for centuries in Indonesia. If there was something wrong with this food, it would have been discovered a long time ago.

Soybeans have many anticancer properties:

- Genistein may stop the spread of some forms of cancer at an early stage

- Protease Inhibitors, universal anti-carcinogen and may block the action of cancer causing enzymes

- Phytic acids, inhibit growth of tumors

Soybeans have easily absorbable iron, many B vitamins, carotin, and support detoxification, promote vitality and feed and nurture the lungs and large intestines. Soybeans made into tofu are high in calcium. When made into tempeh it is 19.5% protein. Containing all eight essential amino acids, it is a complete protein. When made into miso it has 11 g. of complete protein in 1 T. And by fermenting it to make the miso, the healing properties are enhanced. Miso is a living food containing lactobacillus, a healthful microorganism that aids in digestion. There are so many wonderful health benefits from soy foods, I can see why we have been eating it for thousands of years.

I feel there is a lot of confusion about the plant based phyto-estrogen, isoflavones in soybeans. This part of the bean does not disrupt your estrogen levels, it balances them. If you are too low, it raises them, it you are too high it lowers them. These isoflavones also have been credited with slowing the effects of osteoporosis, relieving some side effects of menopause, and alleviating some side effects of cancer. Not to mention it has been shown to dramatically lower the undesirable L.D.L. cholesterol. It is interesting that in China, where they eat soybean products such as tofu, tempeh, and miso every day, that until recently they did not have a word in their language for hot flashes. Of course now, because they have introduced our highly refined and processed way of eating into their culture, that is changing. Also many times a women is told by her doctor to take photo-estrogen pills, for whatever reason. Why not get it from your food instead of a pill?

I do want to say that when buying soybean foods, you must buy organic. It is, right now, our only way to have some kind of insurance that the soybeans have not been genetically altered. And eat the soy foods that have stood the test of time: tofu, tempeh, miso, tamari, and shoyu. Just like any other food, if it has been refined or processed some of the nutritional quality will suffer.

I know there are articles and books out there that give soybeans a bad rep. They quote studies that say it is harmful. And I have come to the conclusion these studies are not reliable. Soybeans have been studied probably more than any other health food. So it is easy to pick only a handful of negative studies, if that is what will profit you, and ignore the majority of favorable studies. And most of these studies are done on animals, usually mice or rats. These animals are feed high amounts of the isoflavones isolated, not the whole soybean. Also they are feed a large amount that is much more than a human would eat. And human bodies assimilate differently than mice, so the reaction cannot be compared. Every one of these that I have seen, excludes the foods I mention above and have been eaten for thousands of years.

Our epidemic of sickness does not come from food that has been eaten for thousands of years. It is from our culture of fast foods, processed foods, microwaved foods, refined foods, overconsumption of sugar and the huge amount of stress we live with every day. Also from the absurd notion, more is better. For instance, if you drink three quarts of soy milk a day, you are going to have some reaction. (This was actually one study that came to the conclusion soy is bad.) That is way too much of any one food to be consuming. I do not care if it is cow's milk, goat's milk, almond milk, rice milk, or soy milk.

Do some research and decide for yourself. But I would not pay any attention to studies done on animals and studies done with huge amount of soy consumed. Up until recently, China had one of the lowest rates of cancer. One of their main food sources is soy and has been for thousands of years. If there was any link with eating soy and getting cancer, don't you think the Chinese would have been dying from cancer long before this. (Common sense!) And lastly I would like to point out there are huge multibillion dollar industries that would not want to lose their business to a wonderful, high protein plant based food source. Maybe some of these multibillion dollar industry sponsored the research?

Macrobiotics

Macrobiotics is a lifestyle that incorporates living close to nature. It involves eating foods that are not tampered with, refined, processed, or sprayed with chemicals. In this lifestyle you eat foods in their whole form. Also incorporated in the lifestyle is eating locally grown and seasonal foods. It is a very healthy way of eating, akin to the way our ancestors use to eat.

The diet is centered on whole grains: brown rice, millet, oats, quinoa, buckwheat, amaranth, barley and corn. These are your complex carbohydrates, what gives your body energy, long sustainable energy to last throughout the day.

This food group is very high in fiber and full of minerals and vitamins. Unfortunately, most people get their grains in the form of refined grains, cereals, flours, breads and pastas, most of which have severely diminished nutritional value.

Also centered in the diet is beans: kidney, pinto, black, white, chick peas, lentils and soy. This is where you get your protein which helps keep you strong. The diet also includes a wide variety of vegetables, naturally fermented foods, nuts and seeds, sea vegetables and fruit. Sea vegetables are a family of vegetables that are the most nutrient dense foods on the planet. They are high in calcium, protein, iron, minerals and trace minerals. They are grown in the ocean and you buy them dried. All these foods were consumed by our ancestors. They ate a wide variety of whole foods and unless they were dried and nonperishable, they ate what was local. For instance, living in Michigan our ancestors would not eat bananas because they do not grow here. Bananas would be ideally suited for people who live where they grow, but not ideal for people here in Michigan. We would be better off eating foods like pears, blueberries, squashes, onions, wild rice, root vegetables and cabbages. Also because we have different seasons here, we eat according to the different seasons. In the winter time we want to eat foods that will help keep our bodies warm. Such foods include winter squashes, hard root vegetables, warming stews, casseroles, thick hardy soups and hot oatmeal. In the summer time we eat more foods that help cool our bodies down to help deal with the heat. We can consume more raw foods such as salads, also fruits are available, summer squashes, leafy greens and cucumbers. Macrobiotics involves looking towards nature. Living a lifestyle and eating according to what nature has provided us and what is available around us from nature.

The macrobiotic lifestyle also involves the study and understanding of energy. Here is a quote from my cookbook, ***Perceptions in Healthy Cooking*** explaining about energy: "I would like to explain a little about energy in our food. Everything is made up of energy. In fact, everything is made up of two opposite energies existing in the same space at the same time. These energies exist in everything in varying degrees. One of the two energies is more prominent, so we can classify things according to the energy that I most dominant, we call these energies yin and yang. Yin energy is expansive and moves in an upwards direction. Yang energy is constrictive and moves in a downward direction. Yin is cold, yang is hot. Yin is wet, yang is dry. Yin is sweet, yang is salty.

In food, we classify foods according to their energies. Picture in your mind a teeter totter. On the left side imagine the yin energy, on the right imagine the yang energy. Foods that have strong yin or yang energies will be at the very end of the teeter totter. In the middle will be more balanced energy foods, where the energies are more equal. One the left (yin) side, would be foods such as white refined sugar, artificial sweeteners, white flour and foods that contain those ingredients. On the right (yang) side would be your meats, (beef, pork, chicken), eggs, and salty snacks (potato chips, crackers). Now if you at these extreme energy foods, your teeter totter will swing back and forth, up and down, going from one extreme to another. Tis creates chaotic energy. Let's now look at the middle of the teeter totter. This is where you find plant based foods.

The yin and yang energy in these foods are more balanced, or more equal. This is where you will find whole grains, beans, vegetables and sea vegetables. If you choose to eat foods from the middle of the teeter totter, wouldn't it make sense that your energy would be calmer? As opposed to the extreme energy foods at the ends of the teeter totter that would create going from one extreme to the other, thus creating chaotic energy.

I find the study of energy extremely interesting, I have briefly explained the basics to you, but there is so much more to learn about this study of energy. There are many books written on this subject: **The Macrobiotic Way** by Michio Kushi, ***You Are All Sanpaku*** by George Ohsawa and William Duffy, **Confessions of a Kamikaze Cowboy** by Dirk Benedict. Please get them and read more about this interesting subject."

Organic and Vegan

I use organic ingredients whenever possible. The recipes in this cookbook does not say 'organic' before each ingredient, however I highly recommend you buy organic whenever possible. Organic means that the food was grown or produced without the use of chemicals. The number of chemicals sprayed on our food has become epidemic. The human body was not made to ingest chemicals. The chemicals that are sprayed on our food have not been tested for their long term effect on the body. We are literally a living experiment. Many people have health issues that can be related to the chemicals sprayed on our food.

Besides the health benefits of eating organic there is the superior taste of organic food. Chemicals are bitter to the taste, and you can tell when you do a taste comparison. The taste difference is most profound in naturally sweet vegetables such as carrot and onions. And try tasting organic fruit compared to conventional fruit. The organic is always sweeter. Because of the high water content in fruit, the bitter chemical taste comes through strong.

All my recipes are vegan. I believe it is a personal decision every person has to make for themselves if they choose to be either vegetarian or vegan. Since I became vegan there seems to be even more research showing how cutting out the animal products from your diet can help improve many health issues.

If you have ever seen pictures of the appalling conditions that animals are raised in for our consumption, you would be turned off of eating animals products. The animals are kept in horrible conditions and fed unnatural foods filled with growth hormones and antibiotic. The growth hormones and antibiotic are intended to make the animals grow faster and get bigger quicker. You are what you eat. Take a look at our culture and you can see the parallel. There are many books, movies, videos and other information about the issue that anyone can do research on when they are ready to know the truth about the food they eat.

Night Shades Vegetables

As a general rule, I do not use night shade vegetables in my cooking. You will not find the typical tomatoes, avocados and potatoes in my recipes. I do occasionally use them in special dishes. Many people have seen dramatic results in the reduction of pain due to arthritis and fibromyalgia, after cutting back or not consuming them in their diets. Night shades contain oxalic acid, which binds with calcium in our body, which leads to calcification or arthritis. An occasional one of these night shades probably will not hurt you, but our modern diets have been geared to include these foods as a major part. Here is a list of night shades: tomatoes, white potatoes, eggplant, all peppers, beet greens, spinach, Swiss chard, avocados, coconut and tobacco.

These night shades also contain toxins. Potatoes contain solonates, and tomatoes contain tomatotine, which are both toxins. And it is interesting to note that tomatoes when first introduced to the Europeans in 1500 – 1600's they got a very cold reception. And white potatoes were considered very low grade food and fed to live stock.

Dairy Products

I do not use dairy products on my recipes. Dairy products are high in calories, and contain saturated fats which can cause weight gain. In fact the main nutritional purpose of cow's milk is to help the baby cow gain weight and grow fast so the calf can run away from predators. Consuming cow's milk can contribute to high cholesterol levels which could lead to fatty deposits in the arteries, and that raises the risk of heart attacks and strokes.

The main reason to stay away from dairy products in your diet is the allergic reaction most people experience from consuming them. There are more than 25 proteins in milk that can lead to various problems such as: eczema, asthma, ear infections, bronchitis and sinusitis. And the growth hormones and antibiotics they force the cows to eat end up in all dairy products. Growth hormones that are identical in humans and cows which lead to humans who consume dairy to mature as an early age. Due to the growth hormones and selective breeding cows now can product up to 50 quarts of milk a day. Whereas 300 years go they were lucky to get one quart of milk per day from a cow.

We are the only species on the planet who consumes milk after we are weaned off our mother's milk. It is not even human milk, but milk from a different species. Once a child matures they are intended to stop drinking mother's milk and start chewing food and they loss the digestive enzymes to properly digest milk. But in our culture we force kids to continue to consume milk after their bodies tell them to stop consuming milk.

My preferred milk substitute is made from rice. In my recipes I call it, rice beverage. There is a specific definition for 'milk' which is why I choose to call it 'beverage' instead of milk. You can use your favorite nondairy milk in any of the recipes. Just make sure to read the labels and stay away from ones that have sugar in them.

Thanksgiving

Tofu Turkey, Whole Grain Bread Stuffing, Colorful Sweet and Sour Kale, Millet Mash Mock Potato with Onion Gravy

Thanksgiving usually is the start of the celebrating of the annual holiday season. Since 1997 I have been hosting my annual, sit down Thanksgiving dinner. I offer a place for my students and friends to come enjoy a home cooked, healthy Thanksgiving meal. I wanted to create a fun environment where people could socialize and have a relaxed dinner without worrying about any of the prep or cleanup of the dinner. And my dishes are all vegan and based on macrobiotic principles. Using whole grain, organic whole foods, no saturated fats, and no sugar, I create an incredible flavorful holiday dinner.

The recipes have basically stayed the same over the years with only a few slight changes. These are some of my most flavorful dishes I cook all year. The Whole Grain Stuffing, has become my family's favorite and I cook and serve it at my family Thanksgiving dinner every year. Within the last few years I created my gluten free, Millet Sweet Potato Stuffing that is full of traditional flavors for another version of stuffing. My Tofu Turkey, is visually impressive and full of flavor with just three ingredients. If you have any left over after your dinner, the Tofu Turkey also make great sandwiches. You can slice it and put on bread along with lettuce and your favorite condiment. Or chop it up with onions, celery and Vegenaise and you have a vegan turkey salad to put on bread for a sandwich.

My Millet Mashed Mock Potato, and Onion Gravy are a staple at this time of year. I use millet and cauliflower to replace the night shade white potato, traditionally served for Thanksgiving dinner. You will get all the rich, creamy taste without the possibility of joint pains associated with the family of night shade vegetables. The palate cleansers for the dinner is my, Colorful Sweet and Sour Kale. Using an apple and sauerkraut in this dish creates the perfect side dish to complement the meal.

I must admit I am not a huge fan of Cranberry Sauce, I share my cranberry sauce recipe in this section. I have created a different fruit dish using two of my favorite fruits, fig and blackberry to create an alternative with my Fig Blackberry Sauce (page 38), which is now my family's favorite also.

Whole Grain Bread Stuffing

8 Shiitake mushrooms
1 cup short grain brown rice
2 cups water
1 onion (diced)
3 celery (diced)
3 garlic cloves (minced)
2 tsp. sage
2 tsp. thyme
2 tsp. marjoram
4 T. tamari
1 T. toasted sesame oil
approx. ¾ loaf of whole grain bread

    Soak the shiitake mushrooms for 15 minutes. Remove the mushrooms and cut in thin slices, removing and discarding the stems. Use the soaking water for the 2 cups of water to cook the brown rice. Put in a pot the sliced shiitake, brown rice, and 2 cups water, bring to a boil for 2 minutes. Reduce to the lowest possible temperature, cover and simmer for one hour. Meanwhile, sauté the onions in toasted sesame oil with a dash of tamari until translucent. Remove from pan, put in a large mixing bowl. Using the same sauté pan, sauté the celery and garlic and add to the mixing bowl. Put some water in a shallow dish. Soak the bread slices in the water for a minutes, break up with your hands and add to the mixing bowl. When rice is done, add to the bowl. Season with the sage, thyme, marjoram, tamari and 1 T. toasted sesame oil. Mix all together, bake at 350 degrees for 20 minutes or use in the Stuffed Tofu Turkey, recipe.

Tofu Turkey

3 lbs. firm fresh tofu
½ cup dark toasted sesame oil
½ cup tamari

    Line a colander with cheese cloth. Cut the tofu in to approx. two inch thick, rectangle pieces. Place the tofu in the colander and press to the sides. Create a hollowed out bowl shape with the pieces of tofu. Put a bowl in the cavity, and place weight on top to press out some of the water. Let it press for about an hour. Remove the weight and bowl. Stuff the hollowed out middle with stuffing. Flip the colander over on a cookie sheet baking pan and remove colander. Whisk together the dark toasted sesame oil and tamari. With the cheese cloth still on, brush some of the mixture over the whole tofu turkey. Bake at 350 degrees for 15 minutes. Brush more of the mixture over the whole tofu turkey again. Continue to bake at 350 degrees, coating the tofu turkey every 15 minutes until it has baked for one hour. After 30 minutes, remove the cheese cloth.

Tofu Turkey

Gluten Free Millet Sweet Potato Stuffing

1 ½ cups millet - 3 ½ cups water
6 dried shitake mushrooms
2 large sweet potatoes (peeled and cut in cubes)
1 (8 oz.) package tempeh (crumbled)
1 T. olive oil - 2 tsp. tamari
½ tsp. each: sea salt, thyme, sage, marjoram
1 onion (diced)
3 celery stalks (diced)
3 garlic cloves (minced)
Additional Seasoning:
1 T. toasted sesame oil
5 T. tamari
1/3 cup tahini
2/3 cup water
1 tsp. sea salt - 2 ½ tsp. sage
1 ½ tsp. each: thyme and marjoram

    Cover shiitake mushrooms with water in a pot, bring to a boil, reduce heat and simmer for 15 minutes. Remove mushrooms (once cooled, slice thin) and use the water for the 3 ½ cups water to cook millet. Put millet and 3 ½ cups water in a pot. Bring to a boil, reduce heat to low, cover and simmer for 20 minutes, until all water has been absorbed. Bring a pot of water to a boil. Put sweet potatoes in boiling water, cook for 10 minutes, until fork tender, and drain, set aside. Put the crumbled tempeh, olive oil, 2 tsp. tamari, and ½ tsp. of each seasoning, in a sauté pan, and brown the tempeh. Remove from pan and use the same pan to sauté the onions, celery garlic and mushrooms, one at a time, in toasted sesame oil and tamari. Mix all together the millet, sweet potatoes, tempeh, sautéed vegetables and additional seasoning. Put in a 13 x 9 inch, casserole dish and bake at 350 degrees for 25 minutes.

Millet Mashed Mock Potatoes

1 cup millet
3 cups water
½ head of cauliflower (cut up)
½ onion (chopped)
1 ½ tsp. sea salt
2 T. tahini

Put the millet, water, cauliflower and onion in a large pot. Bring to a boil. Reduce to lowest possible temperature, cover and simmer for 25 minutes, until all water has been absorbed and cauliflower is soft. Add the sea salt, and tahini. Put in a food processor and puree until smooth. Serve warm with Onion Gravy.

Onion Gravy

4 cups water
½ onion (diced small)
1 tsp. sea salt
3 T. tamari
4 T. kudzu root or arrowroot, dissolved in ½ cup water
¼ cup minced parsley

Bring water to a boil in a pot. Add the onion, reduce heat, and simmer for 5 minutes. Add the sea salt and tamari, simmer for 5 more minutes. Dissolve the kudzu or arrowroot in ½ cup water. Add to the pot, whisking as you add the thickening agent. Gravy will thicken as it continues to cook. Turn off heat once thick, and add parsley.

Colorful Sweet and Sour Kale

1 large carrot (pencil cut)
1 large apple (sliced thin)
1 cup water
1 bunch kale (chopped)
2 cups purple cabbage (diced)
1 T. brown rice vinegar
1 tsp. sea salt
1 cup sauerkraut

Put the carrot, apple and water in a large pot, bring to a boil. Reduce heat, cover and simmer for 5 minutes. Add the kale, cabbage, brown rice vinegar and sea salt. Cover, and simmer for 15 minutes. Add the sauerkraut and continue simmering for 7 more minutes. Mix all together and serve.

Cranberry Sauce

12 oz. fresh cranberries
½ cup brown rice syrup
2 T. maple syrup
½ cup apricot preserves (jam)
¼ tsp. each: cinnamon, ginger, cardamom, sea salt
2 T. agar flakes
½ cup chopped walnuts

Wash cranberries, and put in pot. Add rest of ingredients, except walnuts, to the pot. Cover, bring to a boil, reduce heat and simmer for 15 minutes. Turn off hear, mix in walnuts, and pour into dish. Let cool completely before serving. Store in refrigerator.

Pumpkin Pie

Crust:
1 ¾ cup flour (spelt, oat)
¼ cup each: olive oil and water
pinch sea salt
Filling:
1 can (15 oz.) pumpkin puree
½ (12.3 oz.) package silken extra firm tofu
1 cup brown rice syrup
2 tsp. cinnamon
1 tsp. ginger
¼ tsp. each: cloves, nutmeg, allspice and sea salt
2 T. agar flakes
4 T. arrowroot

    To make crust, mix together the olive oil, water and sea salt. Mix in flour, until you get a firm dough that will stick together. Form a flat round disc, wrap in plastic wrap and refrigerate for 30 minutes. Once cold, roll out crust by placing the dough in between two pieces of plastic wrap and roll until it will fit a 9 inch pie pan. Place the crust in the oiled pie pan and crimp around for a decorative crust. Place all filling ingredients in a food processor and puree until smooth. Pour in to a pan and cook on stove on low heat for 10 minutes, stirring occasionally. Pour the filling in to the pie crust. Bake at 350 degrees for 45 minutes. Let cool completely before cutting.

Christmas Dinner

Mincemeat Pie

Christmas is one of my favorite holidays. As a kid I loved all the decorations, gift giving, songs, getting together with family and the uplifting feeling of love. I still continue to enjoy Christmas by getting my tree early and decorating my house to its fullest with festive lights and pink Christmas decorations.

Cooking was always a part of our Christmas celebrating with a big Christmas dinner and many Christmas goodies. I have spent many years since I dedicated myself to living a whole foods lifestyle to create rich, flavorful and festive looking dishes to serve for Christmas dinner. My family has decided my Tempeh and Millet Loaf, is one of their favorites and it is served at our family dinner every year. The Garlic Sweet Potatoes recipe is a great complement to the loaf and can be made the day before to save on time with all that needs to be cooked on the actual day.

Another favorite is the Wild Rice Stuffed Delicata Squash. My favorite winter squash is the delicata. It has a tremendous sweet taste and when baked in the oven in melts in your mouth like butter.

When I decided to make my version of Mince Meat Pie, I went to the expert on making pies, my grandmother (who this cookbook is dedicated to). I remember her pies were the best, and that she would make a mincemeat pie for the holidays. I called her and asked her for her recipe and how she made her pie. She informed me she would go to the store and buy a jar of mincemeat filling and add apples to it to create her pie. My childhood illusions of her home made pie and unique recipe were shattered. I did my own research and found it is made with dried fruit, fresh fruit, some citrus, spices and a little alcohol. Using some of my favorite fruits, my version has pears and figs in the recipe. It has more ingredients then my usual recipes, but I make it only for our Christmas dinner, and definitely worth the extra work once a year.

Mincemeat Pie

Crust:
½ cup each: olive oil and water
pinch sea salt
3 cups whole grain flour (oat, spelt, whole wheat)
Filling:
1 ½ cups chopped dried figs
1 cup raisins
¼ cup mirin
1 lemon (use the juice and the grated rind)
1 orange (use the juice and the grated rind)
2 large pears (approx. 3cups) (diced small)
½ cup apricot preserves (jam)
½ cup chopped walnuts
¼ cup brown rice syrup
¼ cup barley malt (for gluten free, use ½ cup B.R.S. omit B.M)
2 T. molasses (optional)
¼ cup arrowroot
1 T. dark miso
½ tsp. cinnamon
¼ tsp. each: cloves, nutmeg, allspice

    Mix together the crust ingredients. You should get a firm dough that holds together. Divide in half, form two round discs, wrap in plastic wrap and refrigerate for 30 minutes. Roll out each disc in between two pieces of plastic wrap to form the top and bottom crust. Place the bottom crust in an oiled 9 inch pie plate.
    Place the chopped figs and raisins in a shallow dish and marinade them in the ¼ cup mirin, lemon juice and orange juice for one hour. Take half the mixture and puree in a food processor. Take both the pureed and not pureed fruit and put in a pot. Add to the pot the rest of the filling ingredients and mix together. Heat on low until it starts to thicken. Pour over bottom crust. Put the top crust over pie. Bake at 350 degrees for one hour. Let cool completely before cutting.

Lemon and Orange Peel Candy

peel from one lemon
peel from one orange
(use the left over peel from making the Mincemeat Pie)
¼ cup brown rice syrup
¼ cup maple syrup
pinch sea salt

Cut the lemon peel and orange peel in to thin slices. Place the slices in a pot. Cover the peels with water, bring to a boil on high heat. Reduce to low temperature, simmer for 30 minutes. Drain the peels and discard the water. Put the peels in a pot, add the brown rice syrup, maple syrup and pinch sea salt. Make sure all the peels are covered with the syrups. Bring to a boil, reduce to simmer and simmer for 15 minutes. Let cool before eating. Store in refrigerator.

Recipe note: Only on special occasions do I use tropical fruits. The lemon and orange peel are left over every year when I make my Mincemeat Pie and I created this recipe. The peel is high in vitamin C, Calcium, Potassium and can help alkalize your system.

Lemon and Orange Peel Candy

Tempeh and Millet Loaf

1 cup millet
2 cups water
½ tsp. sea salt
1 (8 oz.) package tempeh
½ onion (diced)
3 garlic cloves
¼ cup walnuts
3 T. tamari
5 T. tahini
1 tsp. basil
1 tsp. marjoram
½ tsp. paprika
1 carrot (grated)
½ cup rolled oats
2/3 cup water

Put in a pot the millet and 2 cups water, bring to a boil. Boil for 2 minutes, reduce heat to low, cover and simmer for 20 minutes until all water has been absorbed. Let sit 5 minutes, stir in the ½ tsp. sea salt. Put in a food processor the: tempeh, onion, garlic, walnuts, tamari, tahini, basil, marjoram and paprika. Puree until smooth. In a large bowl mix together the millet, pureed tempeh, grated carrot, rolled oats and water. Press into a loaf pan. Bake at 350 degrees 45 minutes. Let sit 5 minutes before cutting.

Garlic Sweet Potatoes

2 large sweet potatoes (approx. 8 cups)
12 garlic cloves (cut in half)
1 cup rice beverage
1 tsp. sea salt

    Peel and cut the sweet potatoes in cubes. Put the sweet potatoes and garlic in a casserole dish. Pour the rice beverage over and sprinkle the sea salt over the top. Cover and bake at 350 degrees for one hour. While still hot, put in a food processor and pureed until smooth. Serve hot with the Onion Gravy on page 28.

Garlic Sweet Potatoes

Tempeh and Millet Loaf

Squash Parsnips and Kale in Sweet Sauce

3 cups delicata squash (cut in cubes)
3 cups parsnips (pencil cut)
3 cups carrots (pencil cut)
2 cups chopped kale
2 T. olive oil
3 T. tamari
3 T. ume vinegar
3 T. brown rice vinegar
3 T. brown rice syrup
½ cup water
½ tsp. sea salt
1 T. kudzu (dissolved in ¼ cup water)

In a large pot, place the vegetables (except the kale, to be added later), keeping the different vegetables separate. (Looks like a large pie with each different vegetable a piece of the pie.) Whisk together the olive oil, tamari, ume vinegar, brown rice vinegar, brown rice syrup, water and sea salt. Pour over vegetables. Cover, bring to a boil, reduce heat and simmer for 15 minutes. Add the kale on top of vegetables, Continue to simmer for 5 more minutes. Turn off heat. Add the kudzu mixture and mix all together. The kudzu will thicken the sauce in the pot to create a thick sweet sauce. Serve warm.

Fig Blackberry Sauce

3 cups blackberries
½ cup chopped dried figs
½ cup fig or blackberry preserves (jam)
¼ cup brown rice syrup
½ tsp. cinnamon – 1 T. lemon juice
¼ tsp. each: cloves, nutmeg, sea salt
1/3 cup chopped pecans

Put all ingredients, except pecans, in a pot. Cover, bring to a boil, reduce heat and simmer for 15 minutes. Turn off heat, mix in pecans, and pour into a dish. Let cool completely before serving. Store in refrigerator.

Fig Blackberry Sauce, Cranberry Sauce (page 29)

Wild Rice Stuffed Delicata Squash

4 delicata squash
¾ cup short grain brown rice
¼ cup wild rice
2 cups water
1 onion (diced)
olive oil, tamari
1 cup grated sweet potato
1 cup minced mushrooms
½ cup peas
½ cup rice beverage
1 T. tamari
1 T. arrowroot
Additional seasoning:
2 T. tamari, 2 T. tahini, ½ tsp. sea salt, ½ tsp. sage, ½ tsp. thyme

    Cut the delicate squash in half, length wise. Place flat on an oiled cookie sheet, bake at 350 degrees for 45 minutes, until fork tender. Let cool, scoop out seeds, and discard seeds. Put in a pot the brown rice, wild rice and 2 cups water. Bring to a boil for 2 minutes. Reduce heat to low, cover and simmer for one hour. Sauté the onions in a little olive oil and tamari until soft. Remove from pan and put in a large mixing bowl. Using the same pan, sauté the grated sweet potato and mushrooms in a little olive oil and tamari. Remove from pan and add to the mixing bowl. Mix together the ½ cup rice beverage, 1 T. tamari, and 1 T. arrowroot. Pour in to the same sauté pan and on a low heat, cook until thickened. Add to the mixing bowl, the cooked rice, peas, additional seasoning and the thickened sauce. Mix all together. Stuff the squash halves with the stuffing. Bake at 350 degrees for 20 minutes. Serve hot.

Wild Rice Stuffed Delicata Squash

Delicata Squash

Holiday Goodies

Soft Ginger Cookies with Frosting

Since I was a kid, I have been making a variety of cookies, candies and other desserts for Christmas and giving them away as gifts to my loved ones and friends. When I became vegan and macrobiotic I took some of my favorite childhood dessert recipes and changed the ingredients and continue to make them every Christmas to give as gifts. After creating healthy versions of my favorite holiday goodies, I taught all these recipes to my students in my classes. I substituted the saturated fat, butter, for healthy olive oil or vegan butters, and substituted the refined white sugar for brown rice syrup and maple syrup. I use whole grain flours to make the desserts, oat flour being one of my favorites. Organic spelt flour is another whole grain flour that make wonderful cakes, cookies and pie crusts. Spelt is an ancient grain in the wheat family, but unlike wheat, it has not been hi-breed or changed in any way. Many people who have health issues with wheat, have no issues with spelt.

The Soft Ginger Cookies with Frosting is one of my all-time favorite cookie and hopefully soon will be yours also. I use a small amount of molasses in the recipe to give a little extra kick of flavor and spice. As a kid I loved Shortbread, dipped in a hot cup of tea, the Shortbread melts in your mouth.

My Truffles recipe was inspired by a dream. I woke up after having dreamed about chocolate truffles and thought, I can come up with a chocolate truffle recipe. I remember having chocolate truffles when I was a girl from a store at the local mall. They are one of my most popular recipe and every year my regular customers wait for me to make them. I look for the darkest chocolate chips I can find to make the truffles. On the list of ingredients, look for chocolate to be the first ingredient, therefore not being overly sweet. The Fig Berry Pie also came to me in a dream. In the dream I won the. Best Pie, contest and everyone was going on about how wonderful the pie tasted. I created the pie using my favorites, figs, blueberries and dark sweet cherries.

Soft Ginger Cookies with Frosting

Wet:
1/3 cup olive oil
2/3 cup brown rice syrup
¼ cup molasses (or barley malt)
1/3 cup rice beverage
1 tsp. vanilla
1 tsp. cinnamon
½ tsp. each: ginger, cloves
pinch sea salt
Dry:
1 tsp. baking powder
3 ½ cups whole grain flour (spelt, oat, whole wheat)
Frosting:
1/3 cup Sucanat (evaporated cane sugar)
1/3 cup arrowroot
3 T. Earth Balance, vegan buttery spread
2 ½ tsp. rice beverage

    Put wet ingredients in a food processor and puree until smooth. In a mixing bowl, mix together the wet and dry ingredients. Cover dough and refrigerate for a couple hours until cold. Spoon on an oiled cookie sheet and bake 10 minutes at 350 degrees. Be careful these cookies burn easily. Let cool before frosting.
    Put the Sucanat and arrowroot in a food processor. Process for a couple minutes to break up the Sucanat. Add the Earth Balance and rice beverage and puree until smooth. (Be careful not to add additional liquid, the frosting will become too loose.) Refrigerate frosting until cold. Frost each of the cookies.

Recipe note: For gluten free cookies, use all brown rice syrup.

Shortbread

Wet:
½ cup Earth Balance (vegan buttery spread)
¼ cup brown rice syrup
¼ cup maple syrup
3 T. water
2 tsp. vanilla
pinch sea salt
Dry:
3 ½ cups whole grain flour (spelt, oat, whole wheat)

    Put in a food processor the wet ingredients, puree until smooth. Mix in the dry ingredients. You should get a firm dough. Press the dough in an oiled 9 X 14 inch cookie sheet. Poke a few holes in the dough with a fork. Refrigerate for 30 minutes. Bake at 375 degrees for 5 minutes. Turn the temperature to 300 degrees and bake for another 15 minutes. Cut the shortbread while still hot. Let cool and serve.

Recipe note: If you have blood sugar issues you can use ½ cup brown rice syrup instead of the ¼ cup brown rice syrup and ¼ cup maple syrup. To make Chocolate Covered Shortbread, a variation on this cookie, sprinkle some chocolate chips over the cookies when they come out of the oven. Put cookies back in oven for a minutes to melt the chocolate chips. Spread the chocolate over the whole pan of shortbread. Cut while hot.

Vanilla Pecan Tea Cakes

Wet:
½ cup Earth Balance (vegan buttery spread)
½ cup brown rice syrup
¼ cup rice beverage
2 tsp. vanilla
pinch sea salt
Dry:
1 cup pecans (ground)
2 cups oat flour
Powdered Unsugar:
1/3 cup each: arrowroot, Sucanat (evaporated cane sugar)

Put in a food processor the wet ingredients, puree until smooth. Mix wet ingredients with the dry. You should get a firm dough. Cover and refrigerate for a couple hours. Form into round balls. Place the cookie rounds on an oiled cookie sheet. Bake at 350 degrees for 15 minutes.

Put in a food processor the Sucanat and arrowroot. Process until the Sucanat has broken down. Sprinkle the Unsugar over the warm cookies.

Vanilla Pecan Tea Cakes

Fig Berry Pie

Crust:
3 T. olive oil
2 T. each: brown rice syrup, water
pinch sea salt
¼ cup pecans (ground)
1 ½ cup oat bran
¼ cup oat flour
Filling:
1 cup dried figs (cut up)
1 ½ cup blueberries
1 ½ cup cherries
½ cup brown rice syrup
pinch of sea salt and allspice
3 T. arrowroot
Topping:
¼ cup pecans (ground)
3 T. oat bran
3 T. brown rice syrup

    To make crust, mix together the olive oil, brown rice syrup sea salt and water. Mix in the pecans, oat bran and oat flour. Press into an oiled pie shell. Bake at 350 degrees for 5 minutes.

    To make the filling, place all ingredients in a sauce pan. On a low heat, stir occasionally, and cook until the filling starts to thicken. Pour the filling into the crust.

    Sprinkle the ¼ cup ground pecans and oat bran over the top. Drizzle the 3 T. brown rice syrup over the top. Bake at 350 degrees for 45 minutes. Let cool before cutting.

Chocolate Truffles

Creamy Filling:
2/3 cup rice beverage
4 T. agar flakes
½ cup brown rice syrup
pinch sea salt
6 T. tahini
1 cup vegan chocolate chips
Chocolate Coating:
1 bag vegan chocolate chips

    Put in a sauce pan the rice beverage, brown rice syrup, agar flakes and sea salt. Bring to a boil, reduce to low, and simmer for 10 minutes. Whisk in the tahini and 1 cup chocolate chips. Once the chocolate chips have melted, pour into a bowl and refrigerate for a couple hours until completely cold. Once cold, form into small balls. Put in freezer until frozen. Melt the chocolate chips on low in a pan or melt in a double boiler. Gently roll and cover the frozen chocolate balls in the melted chocolate until covered. Put on a non-stick cookie sheet or on parchment paper and put in refrigerator.
Recipe note: You can add ½ cup chopped walnuts to the filling while it is hot to make walnut truffles and sprinkle walnuts on top.

Chocolate Truffles with Walnuts

Chocolate Coconut Pecan Truffles

Filling:
1 cup brown rice syrup
¼ cup rice beverage
2 tsp. Earth Balance (vegan buttery spread)
pinch sea salt
1 tsp. vanilla
2 cups toasted coconut flakes
1 cup toasted pecans (chopped small)
Coating:
1 bag vegan chocolate chips

Heat in a pan, on a low temperature, the brown rice syrup, rice beverage, Earth Balance, and sea salt. Once it starts to boil, turn off heat. Add the vanilla, coconut, and pecans. Mix all together. Put in a bowl and refrigerate for a couple hours, until completely cold. Roll into small balls, put on cookie sheet that can go in freezer. Freeze the coconut pecan balls until frozen. On a low heat, melt the chocolate chips in a pan. Watch very carefully as chips can scorch easily. Very quickly, dip the coconut balls in melted chocolate, cover completely. Sprinkle a little coconut over the top for decoration. Put in refrigerator until firm. Store in refrigerator.

The **Caramel Corn** has to be my most loved Christmas Goodies. I have been making caramel corn since I learned how to make it in a home economics class in fourth grade. When I changed my lifestyle and was going about converting all my recipes to a healthier version, my family made a big deal about how I could never change my caramel corn recipe because it was their favorite and so amazingly delicious. I went ahead and changed the ingredients, but did not tell them. I gave my annual Christmas gifts of caramel corn out and as they were all eating the caramel corn declaring it was the best and that they did not want me to ever change it, I informed them I already had changed the recipe. They were amazed because it tasted the same. I still make my Caramel Corn every year for Christmas gifts and I have friend who anxiously wait for it all year.

Caramel Corn (recipe on next page)

Caramel Corn

1 cup organic un popped popcorn
1 cup peanuts
Caramel Sauce:
½ cup Earth Balance (vegan buttery spread)
1 cup maple syrup
½ cup brown rice syrup
pinch sea salt
2 tsp. baking powder

Pop the popcorn and put it in a very large pot or bowl. Add the peanuts to the popcorn.

Put in a sauce pan the Earth Balance, maple syrup, brown rice syrup and sea salt. Bring to a boil, reduce heat and simmer for 15 minutes, exactly. If you boil for too long the caramel sauce can become hard. After 15 minutes, remove from heat and quickly stir in the 2 tsp. baking powder. The caramel sauce will expand as you stir. Pour the hot caramel sauce over the popcorn and peanuts. Mix all the together. Make sure to get the caramel sauce all through the popcorn, covering all the popcorn. You have to mix it all together quickly so the caramel sauce does not start to cool off which make it difficult to coat all the popcorn. Spread the caramel corn out on 4 cookie sheets. Bake at 215 degrees for one hour. Stir the caramel corn every 15 minutes. Once done, place in a large container. Once it has cooled, you may need to break up the caramel corn as it tends to stick together. Store in a dry place.

New Year's Eve

Tofu Cheese Ball

New Year's Eve is a time for celebrating! In my family that meant celebrating my parents anniversary and we always had a party at my parents' house. We had friends come over to celebrate in the evening with many snacks to put on the table. The kids would have Air Hockey tournaments in the basement, with an ongoing rivalry with my brother, he and I were the champions. And the kids would go outside in the dark to play flash light tag. My parents' house sits on 5 acres so there was lots of room for us kids to run around and hide in the dark. We had so much fun playing flash light tag outside. Oh, to go back to the days when you were a kid and could play and have fun.

The dishes in this section are intended to be served for parties. For New Year's every year mom would make cheese balls. When I was a kid, I loved cheese. So I have very fond memories of her cheese balls. The Tofu Cheese Ball reminds me of my mom's recipe and every year I make my version for New Years. To make the cheese ball you are basically fermenting the tofu by covering it with dark miso. In order to be sure the tofu does not spoil while sitting on your counter and fermenting, you need to make sure you have covered all the surface of the tofu with the dark miso. This fermenting of the tofu is also used in my Fermented Tofu Miso Sandwiches in the Memorial Day section on page 96. Tofu is one of the best versatile foods because it will take on any flavor you add to it in a recipe. Tofu is 8% protein and contains no cholesterol. High in calcium, phosphorus and potassium.

The Sweet Potato Hors d'oeuvre is a great finger food. Sweet potatoes are high in fiber, vitamin C and A. High in manganese which helps promote healthy skin and bones. Also contain antioxidants, potassium and B vitamins. Unlike white potatoes, sweet potatoes are not in the night shade family.

Tofu Cheese Ball

1 pound firm, fresh tofu
dark miso
¼ onion
2 T. tahini
¼ tsp. garlic salt
ground walnut meal

    Press tofu to get rid of extra water for an hour. Spread a thin layer of miso on a plate. Cut the tofu into thin slices about 1/8 inch thick. Place one tofu slice on plate on top to the miso. Spread a thin layer of miso over the tofu slice. Continue layering the slices of tofu and spreading a thin layer of miso over the tofu, until all slices are stalked. Spread a thin layer of tofu on the sides of the stalked tofu, as if frosting a cake. You want to cover all the tofu with miso. Place another plate over the top to cover the tofu. Let sit on your counter for 12 hours. The miso will ferment the tofu.
    Place the ¼ onion in a food processor and chop. Place in the food processor the fermented tofu, tahini, and garlic salt. Puree until smooth. Lay a piece of plastic wrap out on counter. Sprinkle some of the walnut meal on the plastic wrap. Spoon the tofu mixture on top of the walnut meal, piling it in the middle to create the ball. Sprinkle some of the walnut meal on top of tofu. Wrap the tofu ball in the plastic wrap, forming a ball. Place the ball in a bowl, to help create the ball shape. Refrigerate until cold. Unwrap the ball and place on a plate served with some whole grain crackers. Store in refrigerator.

Stuffed Mushrooms

16 oz. large white mushrooms
8 oz. package tempeh (crumbled)
olive oil, tamari
2 garlic cloves
¼ onion diced
3 tsp. tamari
¼ tsp. of each: basil, thyme, paprika
2 tsp. tahini
lemon pepper
sea salt
Vegenaise (vegan mayonnaise)

    Gently wash the dirt off the mushrooms. Remove the stems form the mushrooms. Cut a thin slice off the round bottom of the mushrooms in order for them to sit flat on a cookie sheet. Save the slices of mushroom to use later for stuffing. Sauté the crumbled tempeh in olive oil and tamari until starting to brown. Place in a food processor the garlic, onion, mushrooms pieces (slices that were cut from the bottom), tamari and spices. Puree until all is finely chopped. Add to the processor the sautéed tempeh and pulse to mix all together. Pour mixture back in sauté pan and continue cooking for a couple minutes. Remove from heat and mix in the tahini. Spoon the stuffing in to the mushrooms. Drizzle a little olive oil over the top and lightly sprinkle lemon pepper and sea salt over mushrooms. Bake at 350 degrees for 30 minutes. Serve with a spoonful of Vegenaise on top.

Kale Sweet Potato Filo Triangles

1 package organic filo dough
olive oil, sea salt, lemon pepper
Filling:
1 onion (diced)
1 cup grated sweet potato
2 garlic cloves (minced)
4 cups chopped kale

    Sauté the onion in olive oil and sea salt until well done and soft. Move the onion to the side of the sauté pan, and add the sweet potato to the pan seasoned with a little olive oil and sea salt. Sauté until sweet potato is soft. Add garlic and kale, season with sea salt and lemon pepper, cover the pan and cook for 15 minutes until kale is soft. Mix all the cooked vegetables together.
    To make filo triangles, take a sheet of filo dough and lightly brush olive oil over the sheet and lay another filo sheet on top. Cut the filo dough into 5 equal strips, short ways across the sheet. At the end of one of the strips, place a small spoon full of stuffing on filo. Folding the filo up to look like a triangle, then fold it over and continue folding it over to create a triangle shape. (Similar to folding it to look like a paper football.) Place the filled, folded triangles on a cookie sheet and bake at 350 degrees for 15 to 20 minutes, until the filo is crisp.

Kale Sweet Potato Filo Triangles

Tempura Vegetables

Tempura Vegetables

A variety of vegetables: carrots, asparagus, onion, daikon, broccoli, cauliflower, mushrooms
organic canola oil

Tempura batter:
½ cup rice beverage
2 tsp. arrowroot
1 tsp. baking powder
¼ tsp. sea salt
2 cups whole grain flour (oat, barley, whole wheat)

Cut the vegetables in pieces, if possible make them all similar sizes. One at a time, lightly steam the vegetables for a couple minutes. Let cool so you can handle them.

Wisk together the rice beverage, arrowroot, baking powder and sea salt. Mix in the flour. Batter should be slightly thick, and stick to the vegetable when you dip them in the batter.

Heat a generous amount of organic canola oil in a pot. Using a thermometer, temperature should read 325 degrees. Dip one piece of vegetable at a time in the tempura batter and then directly in the hot oil. Fry the vegetable until the batter is lightly browned. Remove from hot oil, and sprinkle sea salt over while still hot.

Recipe note: Option to serve with a **Spicy Dipping Sauce**: 1 cup Vegenaise (vegan mayonnaise), 1 T. of your favorite spicy sauce, whisk together.

Pecan Oatmeal Cookies

1 ½ cups pecans
¼ cup olive oil
¾ cup brown rice syrup
½ cup rice beverage
2 T. tahini
1 T. vanilla
pinch sea salt
1 ½ cups rolled oats
2 cups oat flour
30 pecan halves

Put 1 ½ cups pecans in food processor and puree until pecans are ground. Mix together the ground pecans, olive oil, brown rice syrup, rice beverage, tahini, vanilla and sea salt. Mix in the rolled oats and oat flour. Spoon onto an oiled cookie sheet and press down with a fork. Put a pecan half on top of the cookie and press into the dough. Bake at 350 degrees for 15 minutes.

Pecan Oatmeal Cookies

Peanut Butter Truffles

Filling:
1 cup peanut butter
½ cup brown rice syrup
Coating:
1 bag vegan chocolate chips

Mix together the peanut butter and brown rice syrup. Form into small round balls. Put balls in freezer until frozen. On a low heat, melt the chocolate chips in a pan. Watch very carefully as chips can scorch easily. Very quickly, dip the peanut butter balls in melted chocolate, cover completely. Put a peanut half on the top for decoration. Put in refrigerator until firm. Store in refrigerator.

Peanut Butter Truffles

Layered Tempeh and Vegetables Dip

1 (8 oz.) package tempeh
¼ onion (diced small)
¼ tsp. paprika
¼ tsp. Mexican seasoning
1 T. olive oil
2 T. tamari
4 cup broccoli (cut up)
1 carrot (grated)
1 ½ cups Vegenasie (vegan mayonnaise)

    Put the tempeh in a food processor and puree to get crumbled tempeh in small pieces. Put crumbled tempeh in a sauté pan along with the diced onion. Add the olive oil and tamari and mix together. On a medium hear brown the tempeh, stirring occasionally. Turn off heat and mix in the paprika and Mexican seasoning. Remove from pan and let cool.
    Steam the broccoli until fork tender. Put in a food processor and pulse to chop the broccoli up finely. In a 8' x 12' casserole dish, spread the chopped broccoli. Sprinkle the grated carrot over the broccoli. Gently spread the Vegenaise over the carrots. (Some of the carrots may get mixed in with the Vegenaise layer.) Last, sprinkle the sautéed tempeh over the top. Refrigerate for a couple hours until cold. Serve cold with chips or vegetables.

Recipe note: Mexican Seasoning is a seasoning blend made by Frontier Co-Op. Ingredients: chili peppers, garlic, onion, paprika, cumin, celery seed, oregano, cayenne and bay.

Layered Tempeh and Vegetables Dip

Sweet Potato Tempeh Hors d'oeuvre

Sweet Potato Tempeh Hors d'oeuvre

2 sweet potatoes
8 oz. tempeh
2 T. olive oil
2 T. tamari
1 T. brown rice syrup
1 T. water
¼ tsp. each: sea salt, paprika, chili powder
olive oil, sea salt
Vegenaise (vegan mayonnaise)
parsley

    Poke a few holes in the sweet potatoes. Bake whole in 350 degrees oven for one hour, until fork tender. Let cool before cutting. Cut the sweet potatoes in rounds slices, approx. 1/8 inch thick. Put a little olive oil in a bowl, dip the slices in the oil, and place on a cookie sheet. Sprinkle sea salt over slices. Bake at 350 degrees for 10 minutes. Flip the slices over, bake another 10 minutes. Remove and let cool.
    Cut the tempeh in 12 equal slices. Lay flat in a sauté pan. Mix together the 2 T. olive oil, tamari, brown rice syrup, water and spices. Pour over the tempeh slices. On medium heat, brown the tempeh on each side. Remove from pan and let cool. Put a spoon full of Vegenaise on each slice of sweet potatoes. Break up the tempeh and put on top of Vegenaise. Decorate with some parsley. Serve room temperature or cold.

Recipe note: For a fancy version, you can put the Vegenaise in a cake decorating bag and pipe the Vegenaise in a swirl, on top of the sweet potato slice.

Valentine's Day

Tofu Salisbury

Valentine's Day, when we celebrate love. What a great way to break up the long winter with a day of letting the people we love know how much they mean to us. The holiday has origins in the Roman festival of Lupercalia, held in mid-February. The festival, which celebrated the coming of spring, included fertility rites and the pairing off of women with men by lottery. At the end of the 5th century, Pope Gelasius I replaced Lupercalia with St. Valentine's Day. However we arrived at what we now celebrate on February 14th. I enjoy creating dishes that could be cooked for your loved ones along with some of my favorite that I would love for someone special to cook for me on this day of love.

The Salisbury Tofu and Salisbury Brown Rice recipes use a combination of tamari and mirin (a brown rice cooking wine) to imitate the taste of a Salisbury gravy. The savory and sweet sauce in the recipes is complemented with all the garlic and onions. A wonderfully delicious dish.

The Millet Stuffed Sweet Potatoes is a colorful, rich, satisfying dish for your sweet heart. And the Tempeh Pot Pie has all the richness of a traditional pot pie. It is an impressive dish when it comes out of the oven. And even more impressive when you get to eat it. Tempeh is one of my favorite foods. It is high in protein, 19.5% and it is a complete protein. Made from fermented soybeans, tempeh is easy to digest, high in B vitamins including B 12. Plus a great source of calcium and iron.

Chocolate is what most people think of when Valentine's Day comes around. My Chocolate Tofu Cream Pie is one of the best flavored pies I have created. It is creamy, sweet and decadent with a strong chocolate flavor. My favorite dessert combo is chocolate and peanut butter. I have used that combo in my Chocolate Peanut Butter Cookie Bars, a recipe I make very often for my regular customers and for a Valentine's treat for myself.

Salisbury Tofu

1 lb. firm, fresh tofu
sea salt and lemon pepper
oat flour
olive oil
4 large garlic cloves (sliced)
Sauce:
½ onion (diced small)
3 T. tamari
2 T. mirin

    Cut the tofu into 4 equal, thick pieces. Press the tofu in between two plates for 15 minutes to remove some of the excess water. Sprinkle sea salt and lemon pepper on both sides of the tofu. Put some oat flour in a bowl, dip the tofu pieces in the oat flour to cover both sides. Put approx. 1 T. olive oil in a sauté pan, sauté the garlic slices until they are staring to brown. Remove garlic and save for later
    Using the same pan with the garlic infused oil, place the coated tofu in pan and brown on one side. Flip the tofu over and brown on the other side. Mix together the sauce. Pour the sauce over the tofu as it is cooking. Cook for a couple minutes, flip tofu pieces over and continue to cook for a couple minutes. As the dish is cooking the sauce will thicken. Serve the tofu on a plate with the sauce poured over the top and the sautéed garlic on top.

Salisbury Brown Rice

1 cup brown rice
2 cups water
½ tsp. sea salt
2 onions (thin half-moons)
4 cups mushrooms (sliced)
3 garlic cloves (sliced)
olive oil, tamari
3 T. tamari
2 T. mirin
2 tsp. arrowroot

    Put the brown rice and 2 cups water in a pot, bring to a boil. Reduce heat to low, cover and simmer for one hour, until all water has been absorbed. After done, mix in ½ tsp. sea salt.
    Sauté the onions in olive oil and tamari until translucent and soft. Remove from pan and put in a large mixing bowl. Using the same pan, sauté the mushrooms in olive oil and tamari until they are soft. Add the garlic and continue sautéing for another couple minutes. Add to the mixing bowl. Wisk together the 3 T. tamari, 2 T. mirin and arrowroot. Pour into the sauté pan and heat on low until liquid starts to thicken. Add the cooked brown rice to the mixing bowl and pour sauce over all. Mix all together and serve warm

Millet Stuffed Sweet Potato

3 small sweet potatoes
½ cup millet
1 cup water
1 onion (diced)
1 cup celery (diced small)
1 cup mushrooms (diced small)
olive oil, tamari
¼ cup tahini
2 T. tamari
½ tsp. sea salt

    Poke a couple holes in the sweet potatoes with a fork. Place on a cookie sheet, bake at 350 degrees for one hour, until they are soft. Let cool, and cut in half length wise. Scoop out some of the flesh and set aside to use in the stuffing.
    Put in a pot the ½ cup millet and 1 cup water. Bring to a boil. Reduce heat to low, cover and simmer for 20 minutes until all water has been absorbed. Sauté the onions in a little olive oil and tamari until they are soft. Put in a large mixing bowl. Using the same pan, sauté the celery and mushrooms with a little olive oil and tamari. Once done add to the mixing bowl. Put in a food processor the sweet potato flesh, cooked millet, tahini, 2 T. tamari and sea salt. Puree until smooth. Add the puree mixture to the sautéed vegetables and mix together. Stuff the sweet potato halves with the stuffing mixture, bake at 350 degrees for 20 minutes. Serve hot.

Millet Stuffed Sweet Potato

Tempeh Pot Pie

Tempeh Pot Pie

Crust:
3 cups whole grain flour (oat, spelt, whole wheat)
½ cup olive oil
½ cup water
¼ tsp. sea salt

Filling:
1 (8 oz.) package tempeh (crumbled)
1 onion (diced)
2 garlic cloves (minced)
2 cups sweet potato (peeled and cut in small cubes)
2 carrots (diced)
1 cup turnip or rutabaga (cut in small cubes)
1 cup chopped mushrooms
1 cup peas
1 cup water
2 T. tamari
1 tsp. each: basil, thyme, paprika and sea salt
3 T. kudzu (dissolved in ¼ cup water)

    Mix together the crust ingredients and form into two equal flat discs. Wrap in plastic wrap and refrigerate for an hour, or until cold. Roll out one of the flat discs in between two pieces of plastic wrap. Put the dough in an oiled, deep dish, pie shell to form the bottom crust. Sauté the crumbled tempeh and onion in olive oil and tamari until tempeh is browned and onion is soft. Remove and put in a large mixing bowl. Using the same pan, sauté the rest of the vegetables, one at a time, seasoned with a little olive oil and tamari. After each vegetable is sautéed, add to the mixing bowl. Add the 1 tsp. each of spices to the bowl. Using the same pan, heat the 1 cup water, 2 T. tamari and kudzu dissolved in water, until sauce has thickened. Pour sauce over all the filling in the bowl and mix together. Pour into the bottom crust. Roll out the top crust the same as the bottom one, place over the top of the pot pie. Poke a few holes in the top crust, bake at 350 degrees for 50 minutes. Let sit for 10 minutes before cutting.

Pear Cherry Pecan Pie

Crust:
3 T. olive oil
3 T. water
½ cups pecans (crushed)
1 cup brown rice flour
1 tsp. cinnamon
pinch of each: sea salt and allspice
Filling:
3 cups sweet dark cherries
3 cups pears (cut in cubes)
¼ cup brown rice syrup
4 T. arrowroot
pinch sea salt
Pecan Topping:
½ cup brown rice syrup
¼ cup rice beverage
1 cup pecan halves
pinch of each: sea salt and allspice

Mix the crust ingredients together. Press into an deep dish, oiled pie pan. Put the filling ingredients in a sauce pan and on a low heat, simmer until filling is starting to thicken. Pour filling in crust. Put the pecan topping in a pan, on a low heat, simmer for 10 minutes. Gently pour topping over the filling. Bake at 350 degrees for one hour. Let cool completely before cutting.

Chocolate Cream Pie with Cookie Crumb Crust

Crust:
1 ½ cup cookie crumbs
1 T. water
2 T. Earth Balance (vegan buttery spread)
1 T. brown rice syrup
Filling:
1 (12.3 oz.) package extra firm, silken tofu
4 oz. unsweetened baking cocoa bar
3/4 cup brown rice syrup
1 T. maple syrup
pinch sea salt

Mix together the crust ingredients, dough should be moist and stick together. Press into an oiled, 9 inch pie shell for a bottom crust.

Put unsweetened cocoa bar in a pan, on low, slowly melt the bar. Add the brown rice syrup and maple syrup. Stir to incorporate the cocoa with the sweeteners. Put in a food processor the tofu, melted sweetened cocoa and sea salt. Puree until very smooth. Pour filling onto the crust. Refrigerate for a couple hours before serving. Serve cold and store in refrigerator.

Chocolate Cream Pie with Cookie Crumb Crust

Chocolate Peanut Butter Cookie Bar

Crust:
1 ½ cups cookie crumbs
2 T. vegan butter spread
1 T. brown rice syrup
2 T. water
Chocolate Filling:
4 oz. unsweetened baking cocoa bar
½ cup brown rice syrup
Peanut Butter Filling:
½ cup peanut butter
¼ cup brown rice syrup
garnish: ¼ cup peanuts (ground)

    Put the vegan butter, 2 T. brown rice syrup, and 2 T. water in a pan and heat on stove until warm. Mix together the crust ingredients and press in to a 9 by 6 inch, oiled pan. Put in refrigerator for 20 minutes. Heat in a pan, on a low temperature, the unsweetened baking cocoa and ½ cup brown rice syrup until the cocoa has melted. Pour approx. 2/3 on the melted cocoa over the crust. Refrigerate for 15 minutes. Mix together the peanut butter and ¼ cup brown rice syrup. Put peanut butter mixture over cocoa, and swirl the remaining 1/3 melted coca in with the peanut butter. Sprinkle the ¼ cup ground peanut over the top. Refrigerate for an hour. Cut and serve.

Chocolate Peanut Butter Cookie Bar

Easter

Chocolate Easter Bunnies

Easter is the first holiday of spring. After being cooped up in the house all the long winter months, Easter is such an uplifting holiday. When I think of spring, I think of soups and sandwiches. Soups are usually warming winter time dishes and sandwiches are usually summer time dishes. Spring being the go between seasons between the two, why not enjoy the combo for your Easter dinner, or brunch. In my business of teaching cooking classes I usually offer a soups and sandwich cooking class around this time of year. When our family gets together for Easter dinner we try and think of easy, fun recipes.

Dulse is a sea vegetable used as a bacon substitute in my Mock B.L.T. Sandwich. Dulse can be eaten right out of the bag or toasted to become crispy. Dulse is high in iron, protein, calcium, fiber, vitamins: A, E, C, B complex, B 12, and contains phosphorus, potassium, and magnesium. Dulse is known to help strengthen blood and nurtures and supports the kidneys and adrenal glands. Sea vegetables such as dulse go mostly unnoticed by our modern culture, however if you were in a Boston pub in the Irish neighborhood in the early 1900's, you would be served a bowl full of this salty snack.

Ume plum paste is another food that is mostly un noticed, but should be in every household because of its tremendous healing properties. The naturally fermented ume plum paste has a strong acidity that has an alkalizing effect on the body when eaten. It can help stimulate digestion, neutralize fatigue, and promotes the elimination of toxins from the body. Having antibacterial properties make this your go to when you need to kill some type of infection in your body. Any time you feel like you are coming down with a cold, start taking some ume plum paste and it will knock it out right away. It is also great for an upset stomach or any digestive issues. I use the ume plum paste for it tremendous taste. It encompasses all five tastes: sweet, salty, sour, bitter and pungent. In the Mock B.L.T. sandwich I use a little of the paste spread over cucumbers to imitate the flavor of tomatoes. Tomatoes being a night shade vegetable, it is better to avoid them whenever possible. The ume plum vinegar is the salty brine from when they naturally ferment the plums to create the ume plum paste.

Chocolate Easter Bunnies

Vegan chocolate chips
chocolate Easter bunny mold
variety of fillings for bunnies: peanut butter, peanut, raisin, crispy

    Melt the chocolate chips. Either melt the chips in a double boiler, or put chips in a pan and on a low heat, melt chocolate chips, stirring as they melt. Cover the bottom of the Easter bunny mold with the melted chocolate, leaving a large cavity to fill later. Put mold in freezer for 5 minutes until cold. Put in the middle of the chocolate mold one of the variety of fillings. For example, put a small amount of peanut butter in the middle. Spread melted chocolate over the top of bunny. Put back in freezer for 15 minutes until completely cold. Pop out of mold. Use this method to create the different variety of fillings by putting the ingredient in the middle of the bunnies. Store the chocolate Easter bunnies in refrigerator.

Pureed Sweet Potato Soup

6 cups water
½ onion (diced)
¼ cup rolled oats
4 cups sweet potato (peeled and cut in cubes)
½ tsp. sea salt

    Bring water to a boil in a soup pot. Add the onion. Let water come back up to a boil, add the rolled oats then sweet potato. Reduce heat to low, cover and simmer for 20 minutes. Add the ½ tsp. sea salt. Using either a food processor, blender or hand blender, puree soup to get a creamy texture. Serve hot.

Tofu Cucumber Sandwiches

1 cucumber (cut in thin rounds)
whole grain bread

Tofu sandwich spread:
1 lb. firm, fresh tofu
1 garlic clove
1 T. olive oil
1 T. brown rice vinegar
1 T. lemon juice
3 tsp. ume plum paste
½ tsp. sea salt
2 T. dried parsley

    Steam the tofu for 5 minutes. Put tofu in food processor along with the rest of the sandwich spread ingredients, except the parsley, puree until smooth. Add the parsley and pulse the processor to mix in the parsley, but do not puree the parsley in the spread, it will turn the spread green. Put the sandwich spread in refrigerator for one hour, until cold. To create the sandwich, you can toast the bread if you desire. Take two pieces of bread, spread a thin layer of tofu sandwich mixture on each of the pieces of bread. Place 4 slices of cucumber on the sandwich. Put together and cut in half of in fourths.

Tofu Cucumber Sandwiches

Dulse Lettuce & Cucumber Sandwiches
(Mock B.L.T.)

Dulse Lettuce & Cucumber Sandwiches (Mock B.L.T.)

whole grain bread
dulse (sea vegetable)
toasted sesame oil
1 cucumber (cut in thin round slices)
ume plum paste
Vegenaise (vegan mayonnaise)
lettuce

Put a small amount of toasted sesame oil in a sauté pan. Place strips of dulse in the pan. On a medium heat, cook the dulse, for a couple minutes. Flip the dulse over and cook until dulse is crisp. Take two pieces of bread, you can toast bread if desired. Spread a thin layer of Vegenaise on both slices. Place 4 pieces of cucumber on bread. Spread a thin layer of ume plum paste on the cucumbers. (This gives the taste of tomatoes.) Place the crisp dulse on the sandwich. Add some lettuce to the sandwich, put together and cut in half.

Italian Brown Rice Soup

1 onion (diced)
4 carrots (diced)
4 celery (diced)
6 garlic cloves (minced)
2 T. olive oil
10 cups water
4 cups chopped bok choy
1 zucchini (diced)
2 kale leaves (chopped small)
4 cups cooked brown rice
2 T. brown rice vinegar
3 tsp. sea salt
1 tsp. each: oregano, basil, marjoram

    In a large soup pot, put the 2 T. olive oil, diced onions and a pinch of sea salt. On a medium heat, sauté the onions until translucent. Move the onions to the side of the pot, and sauté the carrots in the pot seasoned with a pinch of sea salt. After a couple minutes, add the celery and garlic, continue sautéing for a couple more minutes. Add the 10 cups water and brown rice, bring up to a boil. Reduce heat to low and simmer for 15 minutes. Add the bok choy, zucchini and kale, simmer for 10 more minutes. Season with the brown rice vinegar, oregano, basil and marjoram. Mix all together and serve warm.

Cream of Asparagus and Mushrooms Soup

2 cups rice beverage
10 cups water
1 ½ cups rolled oats
1 onion (diced)
1 lb. asparagus (chopped)
4 garlic cloves
4 oz. chopped mushrooms
1 T. olive oil
2 tsp. basil
4 tsp. sea salt

    Bring the rice beverage and water to a boil. Add the rolled oats. Add the onion, asparagus, garlic and chopped mushrooms. Reduce to low temperature and simmer, covered for 15 to 20 minutes. Add the olive oil, basil and sea salt. Using a hand blender, puree until smooth. Serve hot.

Cream of Asparagus and Mushroom Soup

Vanilla Cake with Chocolate Frosting
(Two, 9 inch round, layer cake)

Wet:
4 T. flax seed meal
¾ cup rice beverage
¼ cup water
½ cup olive oil
½ cup brown rice syrup
½ cup maple syrup
1 T. vanilla
4 tsp. brown rice vinegar
Dry:
4 cups whole grain flour (oat, spelt, brown rice)
4 tsp. baking powder

Put in a food processor the flax seed meal and rice beverage. Puree until frothy. Add the rest of the wet ingredients. Puree until well combined. Sift the dry ingredient into a mixing bowl. Add the wet to the dry and mix all together. Pour into two, 9 inch round, oiled cake pans. Bake at 350 degrees for 25 minutes. Let cool before frosting.

Recipe note: The best flour to use for cake is spelt. I created a light cake that holds together. For a gluten free cake use oat flour. If you have blood sugar issues you can use omit the maple syrup and use all brown rice syrup.

Chocolate Frosting:
1 cup rice beverage
1 cup brown rice syrup
4 T. agar flakes
Pinch sea salt
4 oz. bar unsweetened cocoa
4 T. cold Earth Balanced, Vegan buttery spread

   Put in a sauce pan the rice beverage, brown rice syrup, agar flakes and sea salt. Bring to a boil, reduce heat to simmer and simmer for 7 minutes. Add the cocoa bar and continue to simmer for 5 more minutes. Whisk the hot mixture to make sure the cocoa bar has melted. Pour into a bowl, refrigerate for a couple hours until completely cold. Put the cold, solid cocoa mixture in a food processor. Add the cold 4 T. Earth Balance and puree. Turn off the processor a couple times and scrap down the sides to make sure all is pureed well. Put frosting back in refrigerator before frosting cake. Frost cake, store in refrigerator until you cut and eat the cake.

Vanilla Cake with Chocolate Frosting

Mother's Day

Garlic Vegetable Brown Rice Stir Fry

Mother's day is one of the most heartfelt holidays, because your mother is the first person you bond with while a baby and hopefully stays your safe place to go all your life. I have the best mother. She has been there, loving and supporting me my whole life. She has taught me how to be a caring, loving person. She is the most influential women in my life and she was my first cooking teacher. All the basic cooking skills, baking, boiling, whisking and mixing I learned when I was a kid from my mom. The recipes in this section are inspired by some of my mom's favorite tastes and her personal favorites of recipes I have created.

Mom loves soups and when I created the Split Pea Sweet Potato Soup recipe she had some and just loved the way it tastes. When I was a kid, I remember mom making creamy pasta dishes similar to the Mock Tuna Pasta salad I have created. In honor of my Mom's favorite flavor, lemon, I created the Lemon Cake with Blueberry Sauce. We usually have a lemon dessert for our Mother's Day celebration.

Another special mom in my life is my God Mother, Vivian Bottger, who I call Aunt Vivian. My Aunt Vivian loved my Whipped Garlic and would always ask me to make it for her whenever I saw her. When my first cookbook, **Perceptions in Healthy Cooking**, came out, she would carry a copy with her in her purse and pull it out to show friend. She was a kind hearted soul who I loved and respected. She is no longer walking the Earth and lives forever in my heart.

For Mother's day I always honor all the important women in my life: my mom, my maternal grandmother, my paternal grandmother and my God mother.

Garlic Vegetable Brown Rice Stir Fry

1 cup short grain brown rice
2 cups water
2 cups organic broccoli (cut up)
6 garlic cloves (minced)
4 scallions (cut in thin long diagonals)
2 carrots (match sticks)
2 celery stalks (cut in long thin diagonals)
1 cup purple cabbage (diced)
toasted sesame oil, tamari, brown rice vinegar

    Put the 1 cup brown rice and 2 cups water in a pot. Bring to a boil. Reduce to lowest possible temperature, cover and simmer for one hour. Steam the broccoli until fork tender, 4 to 5 minutes. Put the broccoli in a large bowl. Sprinkle a little toasted sesame oil in a sauté pan, add the scallions, and sprinkle a little tamari over as you start to sauté on a medium heat. After a couple minutes add a scoop of brown rice and a little minced garlic, season with a little tamari and brown rice vinegar. Sauté for a couple minutes until scallions are soft and brown rice is starting to crisp. Remove from pan, and add to the large mixing bowl. Continue to sauté each one of the vegetables in a little toasted sesame oil, one at a time, seasoning with tamari and brown rice vinegar as you sauté. Add a scoop of brown rice and a little minced garlic each time to cook and season as you sauté the dish. Once all is sautéed, mix all together, taste and adjust seasoning if needed. Serve warm.

Mock Tuna Pasta Salad

8 oz. elbow brown rice pasta
½ tsp. sea salt
¼ cup peas
¼ onion (diced small)
4 oz. tempeh
olive oil, tamari, sea salt, paprika, dulse flakes
1 (12.4 oz.) silken, firm tofu
½ cup green olives
½ cup Vegenaise (vegan mayonnaise)
2 T. olive juice
1 T. ume plum paste
1 tsp. onion powder

    Bring a big pot of water to a rapid boil on the stove. Cook pasta in boiling water for 7 to 10 minutes, until soft and done. Drain and put in a large mixing bowl and mix in ½ tsp. sea salt. Add the peas and stir together. The warm pasta will lightly cook the peas. Cut the tempeh in slices, place in a sauté pan, season with olive oil, and tamari. Brown on each side of slices. Remove from pan and sprinkle a little sea salt, paprika and dulse flakes over tempeh. Cut the tempeh into small pieces. Add tempeh and diced onion to the pasta. Put in a food processor the tofu, green olives, Vegenaise, olive juice, ume plum paste and onion powder. Puree until smooth. Add the tofu puree to the pasta and mix all together. Put in refrigerator and serve cold.

Split Pea and Sweet Potato Soup

9 cups water
1 2/3 cup split peas
½ cup rolled oats
1 (4 inch) piece kombu
1 onion (diced)
3 garlic cloves (minced)
4 cups sweet potato (peeled and cut in cubes)
1 ½ cups corn
3 tsp. sea salt
1 tsp. basil
½ tsp. each: sage and thyme
2 T. minced kale

Bring the 9 cups water to a boil. Add the split peas, rolled oats and kombu. Reduce to low heat and simmer for one hour. Puree the soup with a hand blender. Add the diced onion, garlic and sweet potato. Simmer for 20 more minutes until sweet potato is fork tender. Add corn, sea salt and seasonings. Turn off heat and let sit 5 minutes before serving.

Split Pea Sweet Potato Soup

Whipped Garlic

6 garlic cloves
¼ cup olive oil
2 cups Vegenaise (vegan mayonnaise)

   Put the garlic cloves in a food processor. Puree until garlic is minced (chopped small). Add the olive oil and Vegenaise, puree for a good 3 minutes. Scrap down the sides. Puree for another 3 minutes. Serve as a dip and store in refrigerator.

Recipe note: One of my signature recipes that I make all the time, my Whipped Garlic is always a hit at every holiday get together. I was inspired by the white, garlic dip that is served at most Mid-Eastern restaurants. I did my best to imitate the thick, creamy heavy garlic flavor in my version. My Mom has perfected the recipe with a little more garlic in her version. She makes Whipped Garlic at their time share condo in Florida every year and all her friends just love it. People tell me they put the Whipped Garlic on everything. My favorite way to eat it is: as a dip, on toast or bread, as a salad dressing, over brown rice pasta, and on the crust of homemade pizzas. My Aunt Vivian, my God mother loved my Whipped Garlic and I often made it for her.

Two Lentil Squash Garlic Soup

10 cups water
1 cup green lentils
1 cup red lentils
1 (4 inch) piece kombu
1 onion (diced)
12 garlic cloves (minced)
4 cups buttercup squash (cut in cubes)
2 carrots (diced)
2 celery stalks (diced)
¼ cup minced kale
2 T. olive oil
2 T. tamari
1 ½ tsp. sea salt
1 tsp. basil
1 tsp. cumin
½ tsp. coriander

Put the 10 cups water and piece of kombu in a large soup pot, bring to a boil. Remove the kombu, cut into small pieces and put back in soup pot. Add the green and red lentils, skim off any foam that may rise to the surface while the lentils are boiling. While water is boiling, add the vegetables one at a time (except minced kale to be added later). Let water come back up to a boil before adding the next vegetable. Once all the vegetables (except kale) is added, reduce heat to low, cover and let simmer for 20 minutes. Turn heat off, add the minced kale, olive oil, tamari and rest of the seasonings. Stir all together and serve hot.

Fig Bars

Crust:
1/3 cup olive oil
¾ cup brown rice syrup
¼ cup water
pinch sea salt
3 ½ cups flour (spelt, oat, whole wheat)
Filling:
2 cups dried figs (chopped up)
1 cup your favorite fruit preserves (jams)
pinch sea salt

To make crust, whisk together the olive oil, brown rice syrup, water and sea salt. Mix in the 3 ½ cups flour. Mix all together to create a firm dough. Divide the dough in half, flatten to create a square shape, wrap in plastic wrap and refrigerate for a couple hours until cold. Once cold, roll out the dough squares in between two pieces of plastic wrap to fit a 13 x 8 inch casserole dish. Oil the casserole dish, place the dough in the dish.

Put the chopped dried figs, fruit preserves and sea salt in a food processor. Puree until smooth. Spread over the bottom dough. Roll out the other dough square the same way. Place on top of the filling. Poke some holes in the top dough, bake at 350 degrees for 40 minutes. Let cool completely before cutting the bars.

Fig Bars

Lemon Cake with Blueberry Sauce

Lemon Cake with Blueberry Sauce

Wet:
1 T. flax seed meal
½ cup lemon juice
¼ cup rice beverage
¼ cup olive oil
¼ cup brown rice syrup
2 T. maple syrup
2 tsp. brown rice vinegar
Pinch sea salt
Dry:
2 cups whole grain flour (oat, whole wheat, brown rice)
2 tsp. baking powder
1 tsp. grated lemon rind (optional)

Put in a food processor the flaxseed meal, lemon juice, and rice beverage, puree until frothy. Add the rest of the wet ingredients and puree for a minute. Put the dry ingredients in a mixing bowl. Mix the wet with the dry ingredients until you have a smooth, creamy batter. Pour batter into an oiled 9 inch cake pan and bake at 350 degrees for 35 minutes. Let cool and top with the blueberry sauce.

Blueberry Sauce:
1/3 cup blueberries
1/3 cup brown rice syrup
1/3 cup water
Pinch sea salt
1 T. kudzu (dissolved in ¼ cup water)

In a sauce pan, heat the blueberries, brown rice syrup, water and sea salt. Add the kudzu mixture, the sauce will thicken as it heats. Turn off heat, let sit for a couple minutes, pour sauce over the cake. Let cool before cutting and serving.

Memorial Day

Blueberry Carrot Pineapple Muffins

Memorial Day the day we honor veterans, the men and women who have served our country. Originating after the Civil War, to honor and remember those who had died in battle, it first was called Decoration Day, the first taking place at Arlington National Cemetery on May 30th, 1868. It is important that we honor all the brave people who have served in the American Armed Forces.

Memorial Day also serves as the un-official, official beginning of summer. To me that always means time to go to the Upper Peninsula of Michigan for a long weekend. When my grandparents owned their big farm in Carney our family would spend the long holiday weekend enjoying being secluded in the U.P. woods and spending quality time with family. I have many fond memories of my grandparents' farm and being with my family. This book is dedicated to my paternal grandmother who owned The Farm in the U.P. I have dedicated the recipes in this section to travel food that you can eat on long car rides as you drive up north or to your favorite vacation spot.

Roll ups and sandwiches being the easiest foods to make ahead of time and to eat while on a long road trip. A good roll up can be left over dishes put inside the roll up, such as the Tofu Fried Brown Rice and Sauerkraut (page 99). I use the sprouted grain flat bread for roll ups, sprouted grains being easy to digest and high in fiber.

Traveling I always bring my own food and have soup for breakfast. I usually have whatever is in season in my soups and Memorial Day is when asparagus is in season. Asparagus is one of my favorite vegetables. When I moved out of my childhood home at 18, I bought some asparagus, cooked it and loved it! I asked my parents if they had ever had this delicious vegetable. Mom said she did not like it so we never had it as children growing up but Dad loved asparagus. Then my sister has some asparagus and loved it also. Now when we have family dinner together, my Dad, sister and I get to enjoy asparagus. High in folate, vitamin C, A and K, asparagus can also help prevent kidney or bladder stones. Containing both soluble and insoluble fiber, it can also help improve your digestion. It is best to eat asparagus cooked, it contains more cancer fighting antioxidant when cooked.

Blueberry Carrot Pineapple Muffins

Wet:
½ cup water
1 T. flax seed meal
½ cup olive oil
½ cup brown rice syrup
¼ cup maple syrup
1 tsp. cinnamon
½ tsp. ginger
¼ tsp. allspice
pinch sea salt
Dry:
2 tsp. baking powder
3 ½ cups whole grain flour (spelt, oat, brown rice)
2 cups blueberries
1 cup grated carrot
1 cup chopped pineapple

Put in a food processor the flax seed meal and ½ cup water, puree until frothy. Add the rest of the wet ingredients and puree. Sift the baking powder and flour in to a mixing bowl. Add the blueberries, carrots, pineapple and pureed wet mixture. Mix all together. Scoop into an oiled muffin pan and bake at 350 degrees for 30 minutes. Let cool before serving.

Fermented Tofu Miso Sandwiches

1 pound fresh, firm tofu
dark miso
whole grain bread
Vegenaise (vegan mayonnaise) and yellow mustard

    Press tofu to get rid of extra water. Either use a pickle press or put the tofu on a plate and place something heavy on top to press the tofu for an hour. Cut the tofu in to 1/8 inch slices. Spread a thin layer of dark miso on a plate. Place one slice of tofu on top of miso. Spread a thin layer of dark miso over the tofu slice. Add another slice of tofu on top, spread a thin layer of dark miso over tofu. Continue layer the tofu with a thin layer of dark miso spread over the tofu. Once the tofu slices have been all layered, spread a thin layer of dark miso on the sides of the stack of tofu slices, covering all the surface of the tofu with dark miso. (Just like if you were frosting a cake.) Be careful to use only a thin layer of dark miso, so your end product is not too salty. Cover the tofu with another plate and cover with a towel. Let sit on the counter about 12 hours. The dark miso will ferment the tofu.
    Take two pieces of bread, spread a thin layer of Vegenaise and yellow mustard on the bread. Place slices of the fermented tofu on top of bread, put sandwich together and cut in half. Store fermented tofu in refrigerator.

Layer Tofu covered with Dark Miso

Fermented Tofu Miso Sandwiches

Fig Sesame Bars

½ cup sesame seeds (toasted)
1/3 cup walnuts (toasted)
¼ cup sunflower seed (toasted)
½ cup brown rice syrup
½ cup chopped up dried figs
2 T. barley malt (or maple syrup for gluten free)
1 T. tahini
pinch sea salt

    Heat brown rice syrup, barley malt, figs and sea salt on stove in a pan until it is warm. Add the tahini, sesame seeds, walnuts and sunflower seeds. Continue to heat for a couple minutes until warm. Pour into an oiled pan. Completely cool before cutting.

Tempeh Sautéed Onion Roll Ups

8 oz. package tempeh
toasted sesame oil, tamari, basil thyme
1 onion (thin half-moons)
1 large carrot (match sticks)
whole grain flat bread
Vegenaise (vegan mayonnaise)

    Cut the tempeh in to 12 equal slices. Lay the tempeh slices in a sauté pan. Generously sprinkle toasted sesame oil and tamari over the tempeh. On a medium heat, brown the tempeh on one side, flip over and brown on other side. Remove from heat, sprinkle a little basil and thyme over the tempeh. Using the same pan, sauté the onions in toasted sesame oil and a dash of tamari, until translucent. Spread a little Vegenaise on flat bread. Place two slices of tempeh and some of the sautéed vegetables on flat bread. Roll up and eat right away or wrap and bring with you to eat later.

Fried Tofu Brown Rice and Sauerkraut

1 cup long grain brown rice
2 cups water
½ tsp. sea salt
½ lb. fresh, firm tofu
olive oil, sea salt
1 small zucchini (diced)
1 cup sauerkraut

Put the brown rice and 2 cups water in a pot, bring to a boil for a minutes. Reduce heat to low, cover and simmer for one hour until water has been absorbed. Cut the tofu into long strips (similar to French fries). Heat a generous amount of olive oil in a sauté pan, place the tofu strips in the hot oil. Fry for a couple minutes until browned on one side, turn over and brown on the other side. Remove the tofu strips from pan, generously sprinkle with sea salt, let cool and cut in cubes. Using the same pan and any oil that is left in pan, sauté the cooked brown rice, seasoning it with ½ tsp. sea salt. Put the sautéed brown rice in a bowl along with the tofu cubes, diced zucchini and 1 cup sauerkraut, mix together and serve.

Fried Tofu Brown Rice and Sauerkraut

Carrot Sauce over Brown Rice and Tempeh

2 cups cooked brown rice
1/4 tsp. sea salt
1 (8 oz.) package tempeh
olive oil and tamari
1 onion (half-moons)
2 cups chopped mushrooms
2 cups zucchini (half-moons)
Sauce:
3 cups chopped carrots
1 onion (chopped)
4 garlic cloves
2 cups water
1 T. ume plum paste
1 T. olive oil
1/4 cup cooking water

    To make sauce, put in a pot the 3 cups carrots, chopped onion, garlic cloves and 2 cups water and bring to a boil. Reduce to a simmer and simmer for 15 minutes. Drain the vegetables and save the water. Put in a food processor, the drained cooked vegetables, ume plum paste, olive oil and 1/4 cup vegetable cooking water, puree until smooth.
    Cut the tempeh in 12 equal slices. Place in a sauté pan and season with olive oil and tamari. On a medium heat, brown each side of the slices. Remove from pan and cut in cubes. Using the same pan, sauce the onion, cut in half-moons) in olive oil and tamari until onion is soft. Move the onion to the side on the pan, sauté the mushrooms and zucchini in olive oil and tamari in the middle of the pan. Sauté until vegetables are soft. Add to the sauté pan, the brown rice, 1/4 tsp. sea salt, and tempeh cubes. Pour the carrot sauce over everything and stir all together, serve warm.

Carrot Sauce over Brown Rice and Tempeh

Asparagus Pinto Bean Corn Soup

Asparagus Pinto Bean Corn Soup

1 leek (washed very good and cut in thin slices)
1 lb. asparagus (cut in ½ inch pieces)
3 carrots (diced)
6 garlic cloves (minced)
olive oil, sea salt
7 cups water
4 cups corn
2 (15 oz.) cans pinto beans
2 T. lemon juice
2 ½ tsp. sea salt
1 tsp. basil
1 tsp. thyme

    In a large soup pot, sauté the leek in a small amount of olive oil and pinch of sea salt for a couple minutes until starting to wilt. Add asparagus and carrots, continue sautéing for a couple more minutes, until vegetables are starting to release their natural juices. Add the minced garlic and 7 cups water. Bring to a boil, reduce heat, cover and simmer for 15 minutes. Add the corn and pinto beans along with the bean water, continue to simmer for 5 more minutes. Turn off heat, add lemon juice, sea salt, basil and thyme, mix together and serve hot.

Father's Day

Portobello Mushroom Burgers

Father's Day is usually a holiday spent outside grilling. Many fathers are outside grilling and my father is one of the best grillers. The Portobello Mushrooms Burgers is one of my family's favorite and we often have them when we are together for this special day. Mushrooms have a high protein profile and contain B vitamins, cooper, selenium, potassium and vitamin D.

My cooking tip for grilling is to invest in some grill mats. They are thin mats that go over you grill and you cook on them. Your food gets the delicious char from grilling and you can even get those cool looking lines in your food. And they help make clean up easier also. All the juices or marinades from whatever you are gilling will be on the mat not dripping down inside your grill. To clean them, put them in a sink with hot soapy water, scrub and they come clean for continuous use. You can even put them in the dish washer. For healthy grilling, look for the mats to be Teflon free.

My father loves chocolate. The more chocolate in the dessert, the better it is, so he thinks. Throughout the years I have enjoyed creating new chocolate dessert recipes for him. The Chocolate Zucchini Cake (page 112) is one of my best that I have created. The health benefits of chocolate include, helping to improve blood flow, lowering high blood pressure and helping reduce heart disease. Chocolate also contains antioxidants, however the highly sweetened chocolate that most people eat does not fall in to the category of being healthy. The best way to get all the health benefits of chocolate is to use unsweetened cocoa and add brown rice syrup to it which gives the familiar sweet flavor most people want.

My father is the best man I have known in my life. When I was young he worked to keep us safe and give us a wonderful childhood free of worries. I grew up with many extra special things in my life that were simple at the time, but now I realize how lucky I was to have such a wonderful father. I grew up on 5 acres on a small farm. We had a horse, two ponies, chickens, dogs and cats. It seemed like a normal childhood to me, but on reflection, I was very lucky to have all that in my young life.

Portobello Mushrooms Burgers

large Portobello mushroom caps
olive oil
tamari
brown rice vinegar
minced garlic
basil, paprika, thyme
whole grain buns, onions, lettuce, yellow mustard
Vegenaise (vegan mayonnaise)

    Wash Portobello mushroom caps and remove the stems. Lay flat on a tray. Put minced garlic on the caps (approx. 1 garlic cloves per Portobello). Drizzle olive oil over caps. Drizzle tamari and brown rice vinegar over the caps also (more tamari then brown rice vinegar). Sprinkle a small amount of basil, paprika and thyme over the caps. You can marinade the Portobello caps for an hour or you can cook right away. Put the mushroom caps on a hot grill and cook on one side, approx. 5 minutes, turn over and cook another 5 minutes. Mushrooms are done when they are soft. Or you can broil the mushrooms in your over until soft. Serve on a whole grain bun with onions, lettuce, Vegenasie and mustard.

Recipe Note: I do not include measurements for the seasoning in this recipe. When I make this recipe I usually made at least four burgers at a time. I put the mushroom caps on a tray and drizzle the olive oil, tamari and brown rice vinegar over all of them. It is approx. ½ tsp. each, olive oil and tamari and ¼ tsp. brown rice vinegar for each mushroom cap.

Grilled Asparagus with Whipped Garlic

1 lb. asparagus
Whipped Garlic (recipe on page 88)

Wash asparagus and cut the bottom 1 inch off the asparagus. Spread some Whipped Garlic over the asparagus. Put the asparagus on a hot grill. Grill until asparagus is browned and soft. Serve hot.

Grilled Asparagus with Whipped Garlic

Grilled Asparagus & Vegetables in Sweet Miso Marinade

Grilled Asparagus & Vegetables in Sweet Miso Marinade

1 lb. asparagus (cut in long pieces)
1 small heads radicchio (cut in half)
1 yellow summer squash (cut in thick slices)
1 zucchini (cut in thick slices)
4 oz. mushrooms (cut in half)
1 onion (cut in thick chunks)
Marinade:
1/3 cup olive oil
2 T. dark miso
2 T. brown rice syrup
¼ cup mirin (brown rice cooking wine)
4 garlic cloves (minced)
1 tsp. each: basil and thyme
½ tsp. cumin
¼ tsp. each: paprika and sea salt
Garnish (optional) 2 T. toasted sesame seeds.

In a bowl, whisk together the marinade ingredients. Place the vegetables in a shallow dish. Pour the marinade over the vegetables, set sit for 15 minutes to an hour. If cooking outside, heat your grill, place vegetables on hot grill. Lay the vegetables in a single layer on grill. Attempting to grill all the vegetables at once could lead to over loading the cooking space, creating a wet, mushy end dish. Grill until vegetables are browned on each side. Remove from grill and put in a dish to be served. Add garnish if desired. Serve warm.

Recipe note: If you do not have a grill, you can make this dish using a sauté pan on your stove.

Wild Rice Corn Sunflower Salad with Basil Dressing

1 cup wild rice, brown rice mixture
2 cups water
1/2 tsp. sea salt
1 cup frozen organic corn
2 scallions (cut in thin slices)
1 yellow summer squash (diced)
3 radishes (diced small)
1/4 cup minced kale
1/2 cup toasted sunflower seeds
Dressing:
2 T. fresh minced basil (or 1 tsp. dried basil)
2 T. olive oil
2 T. tamari
1 T. brown rice vinegar
1 tsp. thyme
1/4 tsp. sea salt

Put in a pot the wild rice, brown rice mixture and 2 cups water. Bring to a boil for a couple minutes. Reduce heat to low, simmer for one hour until all water has been absorbed. When done, let sit for 5 minutes. Put in a large mixing bowl, stir in the 1/2 tsp. sea salt and 1 cup frozen corn. The hot wild rice will lightly cook the corn once added. Let wild rice cool. Add the rest of vegetables; scallions, yellow summer squash, radishes and kale. Whisk together the dressing ingredients. Pour over the salad and add the sunflower seeds. Mix salad all together and serve at room temperature or refrigerate and serve cold.

Sweet Potato Tempeh Salad

2 cups cooked brown rice
4 cups sweet potato (peeled and cut in cubes)
½ cup peas
¼ onion (diced)
1 (8 oz.) package tempeh
2 T. olive oil
1 T. tamari
1 T. ume vinegar
Dressing:
1 ¼ cup Vegenaise (vegan mayonnaise)
1/3 cup stone ground mustard
1 T. lemon juice
1 T. tarragon
1 ½ tsp. ume plum paste

Bring a large pot of water to a boil. Add the sweet potato and boil for 10 minutes, until they are fork tender. Drain and set aside to cool. Crumble the tempeh, put in a sauté pan, add the olive oil, tamari and ume vinegar. Brown the tempeh, and set aside to cool.

Whisk together the dressing ingredients. In a large mixing bowl, mix together the brown rice, sweet potatoes, tempeh, onion, peas and dressing. Put in refrigerator and serve cold.

Peanut Butter Caramel Chocolate Chip Cookie Bar

Wet:
½ cup Earth Balance (vegan buttery spread)
¼ cup each: brown rice syrup and maple syrup
½ cup rice beverage
2 tsp. vanilla
pinch sea salt
Dry:
1 cup vegan chocolate chips
½ cup chopped walnuts
3 ½ cups whole grain flour (oat, whole wheat, barley, brown rice)
2 tsp. baking powder.

Put in a food processor, the Earth Balance, brown rice syrup, maple syrup, rice beverage, vanilla and sea salt, puree until smooth. Mix together the dry ingredients in a bowl. Add the pureed wet ingredients to the dry and mix all together. Press ¾ of the dough in an oiled 12 x 8 inch, oiled pan, put the left over ¼ of dough in a bowl. Put the pan and bowl of dough in refrigerator for one hour.

Peanut Butter Caramel Sauce
¾ cup peanut butter
1/3 cup each: brown rice syrup and rice beverage
1 T. maple syrup
pinch sea salt

Put the sauce ingredient in a pan, on low heat, warm the sauce until it starts to boil, stirring occasionally as it heat. Bake the cookie bars for 10 minutes at 350 degrees. Remove from oven, and pour the caramel sauce over the top. Take the ¼ set aside dough and crumble it on the top of the caramel sauce. Bake for another 30 minutes at 350 degrees. Let cool completely before cutting and serving.

Peanut Butter Caramel Chocolate Chip Cookie Bar

Chocolate Zucchini Cake with Chocolate Ganache Icing

Chocolate Zucchini Cake with Chocolate Ganache Icing

Wet:
1 T. flax seed meal
2 T. water
¾ cup rice beverage
¼ cup each: olive oil. brown rice syrup and maple syrup
2 tsp. brown rice vinegar
1 tsp. vanilla
Pinch sea salt
Dry:
½ cup unsweetened baking cocoa
1 ½ cups whole grain flour (oat, brown rice, whole wheat)
1 cup grated zucchini

Put the flaxseed meal, water and rice beverage in a blender or food processor. Blend until frothy. Add the rest of the wet ingredients, puree until smooth. In a mixing bowl, shift the baking powder, baking coca and flour. Pour wet mixture in mixing bowl and mix all together. Gently fold in the zucchini. Pour into an oiled 9 inch round cake pan. Bake at 350 degrees for 35 minutes. Let cool completely before pouring Chocolate Ganache icing over the top.

Chocolate Ganache Icing
½ cup vegan chocolate chips
3 T. brown rice syrup
1 T. kudzu (dissolved in 3 T. water)

On a low heat, slowly heat the chocolate chips, brown rice syrup and sea salt in a sauce pan until melted. Add the kudzu mixture and stir for 3 to 4 minutes, until glaze becomes smooth and starts to thicken. Remove from heat, let sit 3 minutes and pour over cake.

Fourth of July

Red White and Blue Dessert

I love summer and the 4th of July celebration happens right in the middle of summer, which makes it one of my favorite holidays. Independence Day celebrates when the United States signed the Declaration of Independence on July 4, 1776. The Continental Congress declared that the thirteen American colonies were no longer subject to the monarch of Britain and were now united, free, and independent states. If officially became a federal holiday in 1941.

July is one of the warmest months in Michigan which makes it a great time to cook outside, something I love to do. Any of the recipes in this section that are meant to be grilled, can also be cooked inside in a sauté pan if you do not have a grill. Plus July is when my birthday is celebrated. Many of the grilled recipes in this section are some of my personal favorites.

One of my favorite desserts is my Blueberry Pie (page 122) and if you are lucky enough to pick some wild blueberries growing in the U.P. that makes if even more special. The wild blueberries grown in the U.P. are the best I have ever tasted. Blueberries are full of antioxidants to help fight off diseases and protect cell in the body. Plus they may help protect against cancer, heart disease, and help boost brain functions.

Corn is the signature whole grain for summer, known for feeding and nurturing your heart and brain. And great to add to salads to add color and sweetness. Cucumbers are one of my favorite vegetables and perfect to help keep your body cool in the hot summer days. Cucumbers are high in silicon which is an important mineral to help your body. The Cucumber Corn Salad (page 121) in this section makes a great dish to serve for a Fourth of July picnic.

The Quinoa Broccoli Corn Salad with Lemon Dressing (page 120) features fresh basil in the dressing. Basil is my favorite herb. It has anti- inflammatory properties, vitamin A and K, magnesium and promotes blood flow. I love the flavor and the aroma. And in the summer I put basil oil on before going in the woods because it is a natural mosquito repellent. It works every time and I smell good also.

Red White and Blue Dessert

Blue Bottom:
2 cups water
½ cup brown rice syrup
5 T. agar flakes
1 cup blueberries
pinch sea salt

White Middle:
1 package (12.3 oz.) extra firm, silken tofu
1 ½ tsp. lemon juice
1 tsp. vanilla
1 tsp. brown rice vinegar
½ tsp. ume plum paste

Red Top:
2 cups water
½ cup brown rice syrup
5 T. agar flakes
1 cup dark sweet cherries (chopped)
pinch sea salt

Put the ingredients for the Blue Bottom in a sauce pan. Bring to a boil, reduce heat to low and simmer for 10 minutes. Pour into a rectangle, glass dish (approx. 8 x 11) and refrigerate until cold and firm.

Make the White Middle by placing all ingredients in a food processor. Puree until smooth. Refrigerate until cold, it will firm up as it gets cold. Once cold, spread approx. ¾ of over the blue bottom. Refrigerate to keep cold. Save the ¼ to decorate the top later.

To make the Red Top, put all ingredients in a sauce pan. Bring to a boil, reduce heat to low, simmer for 10 minutes. Gently pour the Red Top over the White middle. Refrigerate until the top is cold and firm. To decorate use a cake decorating bag and star tip. Place what is left of the White Middle into the bag. Decorate the top to look like an America flag by drawing stars and stripes, refrigerate until serving.

Grilled Romaine Lettuce Salad

2 heads of Romaine lettuce (one to grill, one raw for salad)
1 lb. firm, fresh tofu
½ yellow summer squash (cut in diagonal slices)
½ cucumber (cut in diagonal slices)
½ onion (thin half-moons)
2 pieces sprouted whole grain bread
1 carrot (grated)
2 T. Vegenaise (vegan mayonnaise)
Marinade:
¼ cup brown rice syrup
¼ cup brown rice vinegar
¼ cup each: tamari and water
2 T. olive oil
4 garlic cloves (minced)
1 tsp. each: basil and thyme
½ tsp. paprika
¼ tsp. each: chili powder and sea salt

Grilled Romaine Lettuce Salad

Whisk together the marinade ingredients. Cut the tofu into 1/4 inch slices and lay flat in a shallow dish. Take one head of lettuce and slice it in half length wise, leaving the core in the lettuce so the lettuce stays together. Lay the lettuce halves, yellow summer squash, cucumber and onion in a shallow dish. Pour marinade over all the ingredients; tofu slices, lettuce halves and vegetables. Let sit 15 minutes.

Heat the grill and place the lettuce halves on grill. Let cook for approx. 3 minutes then flip over and cook for another 3 minutes. Remove the grilled lettuce and let cool.

Put the tofu on hot grill and brown on each side. Remove and cool. Then cut into cubes. Put the yellow summer squash and cucumber on grill and brown on each side. Grill the onions until starting to blacken.

Once all lettuce, tofu, and vegetables have been grilled, take the remaining marinade and put in shallow dish. Dip the 2 pieces of bread in the marinade and put on grill. Toast on each side until crispy. Remove from heat and cut into cubes to use as croutons on salad.

To create salad, cut up one head of Romaine lettuce (raw), and put in large bowl. Cut up the grilled Romaine lettuce and place on top. Add to the salad the grilled tofu, grilled onions, and vegetables. Take any leftover marinade and whisk in the 2 T. Vegenaise to create salad dressing. Pour over salad and serve with croutons and grated carrots.

Grilled Tempeh Over Fresh Lettuce Salad

1 (8 oz.) package tempeh
Marinade:
1 T. olive oil
1 T. tamari
1 T. brown rice syrup
1 garlic clove (minced)
2 tsp. stone ground mustard
1 tsp. basil
¼ tsp. paprika
Salad:
organic salad greens
grated carrots
diced onion or scallions
diced cucumber
roasted peanuts
2 T. Vegenaise (vegan mayonnaise)

    Remove tempeh from package, keep it whole and poke gently, with a fork, a couple times. In a bowl, whisk together the marinade ingredients. Put the tempeh in a shallow dish and pour marinade over the tempeh. Let sit 15 minutes. Heat your grill to very hot, place tempeh on grill and brown on each side. When done, let cool for a few minutes then cut into cubes. Take the marinade and whisk in the 2 T. Vegenaise to create a salad dressing. Arrange the salad ingredients on a plate, add the cubed tempeh and pour the dressing over the salad, serve right away.

Grilled Peaches in Fig Sauce

4 peaches
toasted chopped pecans or walnuts for garnish
Sauce:
¼ cup fig jam (or your favorite fruit jam)
1 T. olive oil
3 T. mirin (brown rice cooking wine)
pinch sea salt
pinch allspice

    Cut the peaches in half, remove the core. Then cut the peaches in thick slices, four slices per each peach. Place sauce ingredients in a bowl and whisk together. Place the peach slices in a shallow dish, pour sauce over peaches and let marinade for 15 to 30 minutes. Heat your grill to very hot. Put the fruit slices on grill, cook on each side about 5 minutes or until you start to get a blackened color. Serve the grilled peaches topped with some chopped pecans or walnuts. Also tasted great served with some vegan ice cream.

Grilled Peaches in Fig Sauce

Quinoa Broccoli Corn Salad with Lemon Basil Dressing

1 cup quinoa
2 cups water
1 cup corn
2 cups broccoli (cut up)
1 cucumber (seeds removed and diced)
2 scallion (thin slices)
2 radishes (died small)
1 small carrot (grated)
1/3 cup toasted sunflower seeds
Dressing:
¼ cup lemon juice
2 T. olive oil
2 T. fresh minced basil
½ tsp. sea salt

    Put the quinoa and water in a pot, bring to a boil. Reduce to lowest possible temperature, cover and simmer for 15 minutes until all water has been absorbed. Let sit 5 minutes. Put the quinoa in a large mixing bowl. Add the corn to the warm quinoa and the heat will lightly steam the corn. Steam the corn for approx. 3 minutes until fork tender. Add to the mixing bowl. Add the rest of the vegetables and sunflower seeds. Whisk together the dressing ingredients. Pour over salad and mix all together.

Quinoa Broccoli Salad with Lemon Basil Dressing

Cucumber Corn Salad

4 cups corn
1 cucumber
1 carrot (diced)
2 radishes (diced)
1 T. ume plum vinegar
¼ tsp. sea salt

    Lightly steam the corn for 5 minutes. Set aside and let cool. Cut the cucumber in half, length wise. Take a spoon and scoop out the seeds and discard the seeds. Dice the cucumber. Put in a bowl the corn, cucumber, carrot, radish, ume plum vinegar and sea salt. Mix all together and let sit for 15 to 30 minutes. Serve room temperature or cold.

Blueberry Pie

Pressed Crust:
¼ cup each: olive oil and water
1 tsp. cinnamon
pinch sea salt
1 cup walnuts
2 cups brown rice flour
Filling:
5 cups blueberries
½ cup brown rice syrup
5 T. arrowroot
pinch sea salt

To make crust, grind the walnuts to make walnut meal. Whisk together the olive oil, brown rice syrup, cinnamon and sea salt. Add the walnut meal and brown rice syrup, you should get a dough that will stick together. Wet your hands and press ¾ of the dough into a 9 inch, oiled pie pan. Put the filling ingredients in a sauce pan. On a low heat, warm the filling, stirring occasionally. The natural juices from the blueberries will come out as they cook and mix with the arrowroot and start to thicken. Once filling is warm and starting to thicken, pour in the pie crust. Crumble the remaining ¼ of the crust dough over the top. Bake at 350 degrees for 45 minutes. Let cool completely before cutting and serving.

Blueberry Pie

Labor Day

Apple Crow's Nest

Labor Day, what is considered the last holiday of the summer is usually observed on the first Monday in September. We celebrate Labor Day to pay tribute to the contributions and achievements of the American workers. It was created by the labor movement in the late 19th century and became a federal holiday in 1894.

Most people usually enjoy the whole weekend with the last BBQ's outside or the last three day weekend to go up north. The weather gets a little cooler at night but the days are still usually warm. In my family Labor day meant another three day weekend to go to my Grandparents Farm in Carney in the U.P. of Michigan. There were many apple trees next to the little farm house and my Grandmother (who this book is dedicated to) had vast knowledge about the different types of apples. There is a picture of her holding me as a baby on the dedication page and she is holding an apple in her hand. She knew which ones to use in different recipes due to their sweetness. The sweetest ones were best for pies. The tart ones better for making apple sauce and apple butters. She also used a combination of different apples in her pies also. My Grandmother was famous for her pies. The whole family loved her pies, and none could compare. I remember one apple dessert she would make, she called it, Apple Crow's Nest. It was apples baked in a casserole dish with a dough on top. I believe it was a version of Bisquick, or something similar to biscuits on top of apples. I have created my version of that recipe here in this section. Apples are high in fiber, potassium, antioxidants and vitamins A and K.

This section also features recipes using millet, the signature whole grain of late summer. Millet feeds and nurtures the spleen, pancreas and stomach. It is the easiest whole grain to digest, has a high protein profile and when cooked it is creamy and sweet.

Apple Crow's Nest

Filling:
5 cups apple pieces
½ cup brown rice syrup
¼ cup raisins
¼ cup walnuts (chopped)
2 T. arrowroot
2 T. water
2 tsp. dark miso
½ tsp. cinnamon
¼ tsp. ginger
¼ tsp. cardamom
pinch allspice

Top:
½ cup rice beverage
2 T. olive oil
3 T. brown rice syrup
1 T. brown rice vinegar
1 tsp. vanilla
pinch sea salt
1 T. baking powder
1 ¾ cups whole grain flour (oat, brown rice, whole wheat)

Dissolve the miso in the 2 T. water. Put in a pot along with all the rest of the filling ingredients. On a low heat, slowly warm the filling until it starts to thicken. Pour the filling into a 12 x 8 inch, oiled casserole dish.

To make the top, in a mixing bowl, whisk together the rice beverage, olive oil, brown rice syrup, brown rice vinegar, vanilla, sea salt, and baking powder. Mix in the flour. Spread the top over the apple filling. Bake at 350 degrees for 30minutes. Serve warm.

Millet Sweet Potato Burgers

1 cup water
½ cup millet
½ sweet potato (peeled and grated)
¼ onion (diced)
1 T. dulse flakes
2 T. tamari
1/3 cup tahini
¼ cup water
¾ cup oat flour
1 tsp. basil
½ tsp. sage
½ tsp. thyme
½ tsp. sea salt

Put the 1 cup water and ½ cup millet in a pot, bring to a boil. Reduce heat to lowest possible temperature, and simmer for 20 minutes until all water is absorbed. In a large mixing bowl, mix together all the ingredients. Put dough in refrigerator for one hour. Form into patties, brown patties on each side in olive oil in a sauté pan, skillet or grill. Serve on a whole grain bun with onions, lettuce and condiments.

Grilled Sweet Potato Salad

2 large sweet potatoes (peeled and cut into cubes)
1 large onion (thin half-moons)
¼ cup olive oil
2 T. tamari
½ tsp. garlic salt
2 celery stalks (diced)
¼ cup parsley (minced)

Heat a large pot of water and pot boil the sweet potato until fork tender. Drain and set aside. Put the sweet potato and onions in a large bowl. Add the olive oil, tamari and garlic salt, mix all together. Heat your grill to a high temperature, pour the sweet potato and onion mixture on the grill. Grill the sweet potatoes and onions until starting to blacken. Remove from grill and put in a bowl. Mix in the celery and parsley. Serve right away.

Grilled Sweet Potato Salad

Millet Mock Potato Salad

3 cups water
1 ½ cups millet
½ onion (diced)
1 tsp. sea salt
1 pound fresh, firm tofu (crumbled)
1 T. olive oil
1 tsp. sea salt
¼ tsp. tamari
½ onion (diced)
3 celery stalks (diced)
2 cups Vegenaise (vegan mayonnaise)
¼ cup yellow mustard

    Put in a pot the 3 cups water, 1 ½ cups millet and ½ diced onion, bring to a boil. Reduce heat to lowest possible temperature, cover and simmer for 20 to 25 minutes until all water has been absorbed. Let sit 5 minutes, then mix in 1 tsp. sea salt. Put the millet in a 9 x 9, casserole dish. Firmly press the millet in to the dish. Refrigerate for one hour until completely cold. Remove the millet from the dish and cut into small cubes (to resemble chunks of potato).
    Put crumbled tofu in a sauté pan, add the 1 T. olive oil, 1 tsp. sea salt, and ¼ tsp. tamari. Mix together and on a medium heat cook the tofu for 4 to 5 minutes, stirring a couple times. Remove and put in refrigerator to cool. Mix together in a large bowl the cubed millet, cooked tofu, ½ diced onion, 3 celery stalks, 2 cups Vegenaise and ¼ cup yellow mustard. Serve cold and store in refrigerator.

Cauliflower Broccoli Salad

4 cups chopped cauliflower
4 cups chopped broccoli
2 carrots (cut in pencil cut)
Dressing:
1/3 cup tahini
2 T. ume plum vinegar
2 T. brown rice vinegar
2 T. lemon juice

    Steam cauliflower for about 4 minutes until fork tender. Set aside to cool. Steam broccoli for about 4 minutes until fork tender. Set aside to cool. Steam the carrot for about 5 minutes until fork tender. Set aside to cool. Whisk together the dressing ingredients. Put all the vegetables in a large mixing bowl. Pour dressing over and mix all together. Serve room temperature of cold.
*Recipe note: Different brand of tahini have different consistency to their products. You may have to add a little more liquid to the dressing or may need to add more tahini. The dressing should be slightly thick to stick to the vegetables in this salad.

Cauliflower Broccoli Salad

Breakfast Porridge

½ cup rolled oats
¼ up amaranth
½ cup rice beverage
½ cup water
2 T. brown rice syrup
½ tsp. cinnamon
pinch sea salt
¼ cup raisins
¼ cup chopped pecans

Put in a pot the rolled oats, amaranth, rice beverage, water, brown rice syrup, cinnamon and sea salt, bring to a boil. Reduce to lowest temperature, cover, and simmer for 15 minutes until thick, soft and creamy. Turn off heat. Add the raisins and pecans, mix together and serve warm.

Amaranth is classified as a whole grain. It is the very small seeds of the amaranth plant, related to spinach and quinoa. Where amaranth is consumed as a part of the diet, there is no mal-nutrition because of its nutritional profile. High in fiber, protein, calcium, iron, potassium, magnesium, Vitamins A, B6, K, C, folate and riboflavin.

Breakfast Porridge

Apple Blueberry Crisp

Apple Blueberry Crisp

4 cups apples (peeled and cut up)
2 cups blueberries
½ cup brown rice syrup
¼ cup arrowroot
¼ cup water
1 tsp. cinnamon
Pinch sea salt
Topping:
¼ cup olive oil
¼ cup brown rice syrup
1 tsp. cinnamon
pinch sea salt
2 cups rolled oats

    Put in a pot the apples, blueberries, ½ cup brown rice syrup, arrowroot, water, cinnamon and sea salt. On a low heat, warm the filling for a couple minutes. As the filling starts to get hot, stir the filling. Once the filling is starting to thicken, pour into an 8 x 11 inch, oiled casserole dish. Mix together the topping ingredients. Crumble the topping over the filling. Bake at 350 degrees for 20 minutes. Let cool before serving.

Halloween

Pumpkin Spice Oatmeal Cookies

When you start seeing pumpkins everywhere, you know it is Halloween time. The temperature starts to cool down, all the colorful leaves fall from the trees and we take part in an ancient celebration of our ancestors. Halloween's origins date back to the ancient Celtic festival of Samhain (pronounced sow-in). The Celts, who lived 2,000 years ago in the area that is now Ireland, the United Kingdom and northern France, celebrated their new year on November first. At the end of summer, the Celts thought the barrier between our world and the world of ghosts and spirits got really thin. Part of the celebration would be people lighting bonfires and wearing costumes to ward off ghosts. To outsmart these ghostly beings, people would put on masks when they left their homes after dark so that the ghosts would think they were fellow spirits.

Every year abound October I have customers who start asking for pumpkin flavored desserts. Very versatile, I have used pumpkin in many sweet dessert recipes, plus created many savory pumpkin dishes. It is in the winter squash family of vegetables. Pumpkin is high in fiber making it a great food for heart health. High in beta-carotene, a carotenoid that turns into Vitamin A in your body, which can help your body fight off infections and strengthen your immunity. Pumpkin also contains lutein and zeaxanthin, compounds that help protect your eyes from macular degeneration and cataracts. This incredibly healthy vegetable also contains, potassium, manganese, iron, phosphorus, zinc, magnesium, vitamin C, E and several B.

Pumpkin used in baked goods such as cookies or muffins, give an incredibly moist texture and tremendous flavor. If you use fresh pumpkin, instead of canned pureed pumpkin, look for the small pie pumpkin. They are small, sweeter and have a better overall flavor. Leave the large pumpkins for the decorative carving. Simply cut them in half, lay flat side down on an oiled cookie sheet and bake at 350 degrees for 45 minutes until fork tender. Let cool, then scoop out the flesh and puree for a smooth texture.

Pumpkin Spice Oatmeal Cookies

½ cup dried apricots
1 cup pumpkin puree
¼ cup olive oil
¾ cup brown rice syrup
2 tsp. cinnamon
¼ tsp. ginger
¼ tsp. allspice
¼ tsp. cloves
pinch sea salt
1 ½ cups rolled oats
2 cups oat flour
raisins for decoration

    Put in a food processor the apricots, pumpkin puree, olive oil, brown rice syrup, spices and sea salt. Puree to chop up the apricots into small pieces. Put in a mixing bowl the rolled oats and oat four. Add the puree mixture to the mixing bowl and mix all together. Spoon the dough onto an oiled cookies sheet. Press cookies down with a fork. Decorate the cookies with raisins to create faces on the cookies. Bake at 350 degrees for 15 minutes. Let cool before eating.

Pumpkin Hummus

½ cup dried chickpeas or one (15 oz. can)
1 inch kombu
1 ½ cups pumpkin puree
1 cup baked sweet potato puree
3 garlic cloves
½ cup tahini
¼ cup lemon juice
¼ cup water
1 T. fresh grated turmeric (or 1 tsp. dried)
½ tsp. cinnamon
1 tsp. sea salt
¼ tsp. ginger
¼ tsp. cloves

    Soak dried chick peas for 8 to 10 hours. Drain and rinse chickpeas. Discard soaking water. Put chick peas, kombu and fresh water in a pot. Add enough water to cover chick peas with a couple inches of water on top. Bring to a boil. Reduce to a simmer, cover and simmer for an hour and a half, until chick peas are soft. Drain chick peas. If you use the can chick peas, just drain the chick peas.
    Put garlic in food processor and chop up small. Add the chick peas, pumpkin, sweet potato, lemon juice, and water, puree until smooth. Add the turmeric, sea salt, ginger and cloves. Continue pureeing for another few minutes until all combined and smooth. Serve with vegetables or crackers. Store in refrigerator.

Recipe note: To make sweet potato puree, bake a sweet potato in oven at 350 degrees for one hour until soft. Take skin off and put in food processor, puree until smooth.

Creamy Pureed Pumpkin Soup

4 cups water
2 cups rice beverage
1 onion (diced)
4 cups pumpkin puree
2 cups cooked brown rice
2 tsp. sea salt
½ tsp. fresh grated turmeric
½ tsp. cumin
¼ tsp. chili powder

    Bring water and rice beverage to a boil in a soup pot. Add onions. Add pumpkin and cooked brown rice. Reduce heat to low, cover and simmer for 20 minutes. Turn off heat, add sea salt, cumin, chili powder and turmeric. Puree soup, either use a hand blender, food processor or blender. Serve hot.

    Turmeric is an incredible spice used in India for thousands of years. When using it in savory dishes it combines very well with cumin. When using it in sweet dishes it combines with cinnamon very well. Turmeric has an abundance of healing properties: antiseptic, anti-bacterial, anti-cancer and is the strongest anti-inflammatory food in the planet. Turmeric has been shown to have strong pain relieving properties and has helped many people who suffer with pain from arthritis. It also helps detoxify the liver, helps with digestive problems and helps regulate blood sugar levels. I prefer the fresh over the dry, but both are great to use. If using the fresh you need twice as much as the dried to achieve the same taste.

Pumpkin Muffins

Wet:
1 cup rice beverage
1 T. flax seed meal
1 cup pumpkin puree
¼ cup brown rice syrup
¼ cup maple syrup
2 tsp. brown rice vinegar
1 tsp. cinnamon
½ tsp. ginger
½ tsp. cloves
pinch sea salt
Dry:
3 cups whole grain flour (oat, spelt, brown rice)
2 tsp. baking powder

Put in a food processor the flax seed meal and rice beverage. Puree until frothy. Add the rest of the wet ingredients and puree. Sift the dry ingredients in a mixing bowl. Mix together the wet and dry ingredients. Scoop into an oiled muffin pan. Bake at 350 degrees for 25 minutes. Let cool before serving. You can add ¼ cup each, raisins or chopped walnuts to this recipe.

Pumpkin Muffins

Kasha Tofu Patties

Kasha Tofu Patties

1 cup kasha
2 ½ cups water
1 cup chopped mushrooms
½ cup parsley
½ onion (diced)
2 garlic cloves
½ lb. firm, fresh tofu
3 T. tamari
2 T. tahini
1 tsp. sea salt
1 tsp. paprika
½ tsp. cumin
¼ tsp. turmeric
½ cup oat flour

    Put the 1 cup kasha and 2 ½ cups water in a pot. Bring to a boil for a minute, reduce heat to low, cover and simmer for 20 to 25 minutes until all water has been absorbed.
    Put the 1 cup mushroom in a food processor and chop up very small. Put in a mixing bowl. Chop the ½ cup parsley the same way and add to the bowl. Put the 2 garlic cloves in food processor and chop up very small. Add the tofu, tamari, tahini, sea salt, paprika, cumin and turmeric to the processor and puree until a smooth consistency. Add to the bowl along with the ½ diced onion and ½ cup oat flour. Mix all together and refrigerate for one hour until cold. Form into patties, in a sauté pan or griddle heat a little olive oil, brown the patties on each side. Serve on a whole grain bun as a burger or serve with Onion Gravy on page 28 as a main dish.

Sweet Ginger Root Vegetable Stew

1 sweet potato (peeled, cut in cubes)
2 cups carrots (cut in chunks)
2 cups rutabaga (cut in chunks)
2 cup daikon (cut in chunks)
1 cup water
1 tsp. sea salt
1 T. mirin (brown rice cooking wine)
2 T. ginger juice
1 T. minced kale
¼ tsp. cardamom
1 T. kudzu (dissolved in ¼ cup water)

    In a large pot, put each of the vegetables in their own compartments, like pieces of pies. Having the different vegetables in their own separate space helps bring out the flavors of the individual vegetable making the whole dish more flavorful. Add the 1 cup water, bring to a boil. Reduce heat to low, cover and simmer for 15 minutes. Add the kale and seasonings: sea salt, mirin, cardamom and ginger juice. Add the dissolved kudzu mixture and stir as the kudzu thickens the liquid in the pot to create the stew. Serve warm.

Pumpkin Lasagna

1 box (10 oz.) brown rice lasagna pasta
Tempeh Layer:
1 pk. (8oz.) tempeh (crumbled)
2 T. each: olive oil and tamari
1 small onion (diced)
¾ cup mushrooms (chopped small)
2 garlic cloves (minced)
olive oil, tamari
½ tsp. each: basil, oregano and paprika
Tofu Layer:
½ lb. fresh, firm tofu (crumbled)
2 tsp. each: olive oil and lemon juice
½ tsp. sea salt
Pumpkin Sauce:
4 cups pumpkin puree
1 garlic clove
4 T. water
2 T. olive oil
2 tsp. ume plum paste
½ tsp. sea salt
White Cheesy Sauce:
2 cups rice beverage
2 T. arrowroot
1 tsp. sea salt
½ cup Vegenaise
½ cup shredded mozzarella flavor vegan cheese

Bring a large pot of water to a boil. Put the lasagna pasta in boiling water. On a high heat, boil the pasta for approx. 7 minutes until soft. Remove from hot water, set aside to use later.

To create Tempeh Layer, put the crumbled tempeh in a sauté pan with olive oil and tamari. On a medium heat, start to brown the tempeh. Add the onions after a few minutes. After a couple minutes add the mushrooms. Continue sautéing until onion are soft. Add the spices, set aside to use later.

To make the Tofu Layer, mix together all the ingredients and set aside to use later.

To create Pumpkin Sauce, put garlic clove in food processor and chop very small. Add the rest of the ingredients and puree until smooth, set aside to use later

To create White Cheesy Sauce, dissolve the arrowroot in the rice beverage. Put in a sauce pan along with the sea salt, heat on low until it starts to thicken. Once it is hot and thickened, add the Vegnaise and shredded vegan cheese. Whisk together and set aside to use later.

To assemble the Lasagna, oil a large, 14 x 9 inch, casserole dish. Spread a small amount of the Pumpkin Sauce over the bottom of dish. Put a single layer of lasagna noodles in dish. Put 1/3 of the tempeh sauté over the pasta. Sprinkle 1/3 of the tofu mixture nest. Spread some of the Pumpkin Sauce over the top, and drizzle 1/3 of the white sauce over layer. Continue layering to create three layers. End the top with white cheesy sauce. Cover and bake at 350 degrees for 45 minutes. Uncover and continue baking for 15 more minutes. Let Lasagna sit for 7 to 10 minutes before cutting and serving.

Pumpkin Lasagna

Glossary

Agar flakes – sea vegetable in flake form, used to gel liquids
Al Dente – cooked for a short period of time so food is still crisp
Almond Butter – almonds crushed into a smooth paste
Amaranth – small signature whole grain of summer, high in calcium, iron, potassium, protein, Vitamin A, B6, K, C
Arame – black, shredded sea vegetable, high in calcium and protein
Arrowroot – white powder that is used to thicken sauces and desserts
Barley – the signature whole grain of spring, helps break down fat in your system
Barley malt – whole grain sweetener made from barley, will not spike blood sugar
Brown rice – signature whole grain of fall, nutritional superior to white rice
Brown rice syrup – whole grain sweetener made from whole brown rice, best sugar substitute, does not spike blood sugar
Brown rice vinegar – gently tart, sweet vinegar made from fermented whole brown rice
Chick peas – also known as garbanzo beans, creamy, sweet bean high in vitamin C
Daikon – long, white, root vegetable, in the radish family, not as pungent tasting as red radish
Dulse – purple, reddish sea vegetable, high in iron and helps strengthen the adrenal glands
Flaxseed meal – ground up flax seeds, used as an egg substitute in desserts help the rising action
Green Lentils – small, green bean from the legume family, high in protein, calcium, and fiber
Kale – leafy, green vegetable, high in vitamin C, calcium, iron and protein
Kasha – signature whole grain of winter, the kasha kernel is ground up and becomes buckwheat flour

Kombu – dark green sea vegetable, always used in cooking beans to make them more digestible and help eliminate gas
Kombu – thick root that is sold in white chunks, used to thicken sauces, very medicinal and helps to alkalize your system
Maple syrup – natural sweetener used as a sugar replacement
Millet – signature whole grain of late summer, small, yellow kernels, creamy texture
Miso – naturally fermented soybean paste, salty seasoning, very medicinal
Dark miso – fermented for at least two years, darker in color and stronger salty taste
Mello miso – fermented for only one year, lighter in color and sweeter to the taste
Pot boil - to boil in pot on stove with lid on
Quinoa – signature whole grain of summer, high in protein, supports heart and brain
Radicchio – small red head of lettuce
Rice beverage – non-dairy beverage make from brown rice (rice milk)
Sea salt – salt that has not been refined and retains all its minerals and trace minerals
Sea vegetables – sea weeds grown in the ocean, the most nutrient dense food on the planet
Silken tofu – tofu that has a smooth texture, used to make desserts
Sucanat – evaporated cane sugar, does contain some minerals
Tahini – paste made form ground sesame seeds
Tamari – wheat free, salty condiment, make from naturally fermented soybeans (healthy version of soy sauce)
Tempeh – textured, soy food, make from fermented soybeans, high in protein
Toasted sesame oil – unrefined, pure pressed, sesame oil that has a smoky or toasted flavor
Tofu – white, soy food, high in protein and calcium
Ume plum paste – umeboshi plum paste, thick, red paste make from naturally fermented plums, Japanese salty condiment, very medicinal
Ume vinegar – salty brine form making the ume plum paste
Vegenaise – dairy free, sugar free, vegan mayonnaise
Wild rice – wild seed, considered a whole grain

Index

Amaranth	3
Apple Blueberry Crisp	130
Apple Crow's Nest	123
Arsenic in brown rice	9
Asparagus Pinto Bean Soup	100
Author page	VIII
Barley	4
Blueberry Carrot Pineapple Muffins	93
Blueberry Pie	120
Breakfast Porridge	128
Brown Rice	4
Brown Rice Syrup	12
Caramel Corn	48
Carrot Sauce over Brown Rice and Tempeh	98
Cauliflower Broccoli Salad	127
Chocolate Coconut Pecan Truffles	46
Chocolate Cream Pie with Cookie Crumb Crust	69
Chocolate Peanut Butter Cookie Bar	70
Chocolate Truffles	45
Chocolate Zucchini Cake with Chocolate Ganache Icing	110
Christmas Dinner	29
Colorful Sweet and Sour Kale	27
Corn	5
Cranberry Sauce	27
Cream of Asparagus and Mushroom Soup	78
Creamy Pureed Pumpkin Soup	135
Cucumber Corn Salad	119
Dairy	20
Delicata squash	38
Dulse Lettuce and Cucumber Sandwiches (Mock B.L.T.)	76
Easter	71
Easter Bunnies	73
Fats	11
Father's Day	101
Fermented Tofu Sandwiches	94

Fig Bars	88
Fig Berry Pie	44
Fig Blackberry Sauce	36
Fig Sesame Bars	96
Fourth of July	111
Fried Tofu Brown Rice and Sauerkraut	97
Garlic Sweet Potatoes	34
Garlic Vegetable Brown Rice Stir Fry	83
Glossary	142
Gluten Free Millet Sweet Potato Stuffing	25
Grilled Asparagus and Vegetables in Sweet Miso Marinade	105
Grilled Asparagus with Whipped Garlic	104
Grilled Peaches in Fig Sauce	117
Grilled Romaine Lettuce Salad	114
Grilled Sweet Potato Salad	125
Grilled Tempeh over Fresh Lettuce Salad	116
Halloween	131
Holiday Goodies	39
Introduction	1
Italian Brown Rice Soup	77
Kale Sweet Potato Fillo Triangles	53
Kasha	6
Kasha Tofu Patties	138
Labor Day	121
Layered Tempeh and Vegetable Dip	58
Lemon Cake with Blueberry Sauce	90
Lemon Orange Peel Candy	32
Macrobiotics	15
Memorial Day	91
Millet	6
Millet Mashed Mock Potatoes	26
Millet Mock Potato Salad	126
Millet Stuffed Sweet Potato	65
Millet Sweet Potato Burgers	124
Mincemeat Pie	31
Mock Tuna Pasta Salad	84
Mother's Day	81

New Years Eve	49
Night Shade Vegetables	19
Onion Gravy	26
Organic	18
Peanut Butter Caramel Chocolate Chip Cookie Bar	108
Peanut Butter Truffles	57
Pear Cherry Pecan Pie	68
Pecan Oatmeal Cookies	56
Portobello Mushroom Burgers	103
Protein Foods	11
Pumpkin Hummus	134
Pumpkin Lasagna	140
Pumpkin Muffins	136
Pumpkin Pie	28
Pumpkin Spice Oatmeal Cookies	133
Pureed Sweet Potato Soup	73
Quinoa	7
Quinoa Broccoli Corn Salad with Lemon Basil Dressing	118
Red White and Blue Dessert	113
Rolled Oats	12
Salisbury Brown Rice	64
Salisbury Tofu	63
Shortbread	42
Soft Ginger Cookies with Frosting	41
Soy, the truth	13
Spelt	8
Split Peas Sweet Potato Soup	85
Squash Parsnips and Kale	35
Stuffed Mushrooms	52
Sweet Ginger Root Vegetable Stew	139
Sweet Potato Tempeh Hors d'oeuvre	60
Sweet Potato Tempeh Salad	107
Table of Contents	V
Tempeh Pot Pie	67
Tempeh and Millet Loaf	33
Tempeh and Sauteed Onion Roll Up	96
Tempura Vegetables	55

Thanksgiving	21
Tofu Cheese Ball	51
Tofu Cucumber Sandwiches	74
Tofu Turkey	24
Two Lentil Squash Garlic Soup	87
Valentine's Day	61
Vanilla Cake with Chocolate Frosting	79
Vanilla Pecan Tea Cakes	73
Vegan	18
Whipped Garlic	86
Whole Grain Bread Stuffing	23
Whole grains	2
Whole wheat	8
Wild Rice Corn Sunflower Salad with Basil Dressing	106
Wild Rice Stuffed Delicata Squash	37

Made in the USA
Monee, IL
29 December 2022